Raechel's EYEs

Volume II

Raechel's EYEs
Volume II

compiled evidence of a
human-alien hybrid

Helen Littrell

and

Jean Bilodeaux

Wild Flower Press
P.O. Box 1429
Columbus, NC 28722

Library of Congress Cataloging-in-Publication Data
Littrell, Helen E.
Raechel's eyes : compiled evidence of a human-alien hybrid/
Helen Littrell and Jean Bilodeaux -- 1st ed.
p. cm. -- (Star kids chronicles ; v. 2)
ISBN 1-930724-04-7 (volume two, pbk. : alk. paper)
1. Human-alien encounters--United States. 2. Nadien, Raechel.
I. Bilodeaux, Jean. II. Title. III. Series.
BF2050.L58 2004
001.942--dc22
2004026012

The Star Kids Chronicles, Volume II

Manuscript Editor: Brian L. Crissey
Manuscript designer: Pamela Meyer

Author contacts:
Helen Littrell helen5thworld@aol.com
Jean Bilodeaux jeanb@hdo.net

Printed in the United States of America.

Address all inquiries to:
Wild Flower Press
an imprint of Granite Publishing
P.O. Box 1429
Columbus, NC 28722

Order via orders@5thworld.com
or visit http://5thworld.com/Raechel

Table of Contents

Table of Figures vi

Preface to Volume II 1

Introduction 3

03/28/98: First Regression
with Dr. June Steiner and Helen 7

03/28/98: Second Regression
with Dr. June Steiner and Helen 33

03/29/98: Third Regression
with Dr. June Steiner and Helen 66

03/29/98: Fourth Regression
with Dr. June Steiner and Helen 77

Raechel Is Described By The People Who Met Her 91

Trigger Events—Eyes and Windows 99

The Humanization Project 115

The Colonel, Helen, and the Underground Base 120

Helen, Her Mother, and Her Aunt 129

Helen's Pregnancies 134

Raechel's Origin 140

The Blue Lights 147

Men In Black 161

Projects and Agencies 164

Symbols 167

Marisa 169

Contact With Marisa, Raechel And The Colonel 176

Currently Occurring Paranormal Events 180

Epilogue 199

Table of Figures

Figure 1. Drawing of Raechel as Helen remembers her from their initial meeting. 11

Figure 2. Drawing of the place Raechel took Helen during a visit to the girls' apartment. The * marks the spot where Raechel and Helen touched fingers, allowing Helen to pass through the windows and follow Raechel. 19

Figure 3. A drawing of the Christmas bird that alerted Helen and author Jean Bilodeaux that something strange was happening. 22

Figure 4. Triangular emblem seen on Raechel's food and water containers, on the license plate of the car driven by the men visiting Raechel at her apartment, and on a truck outside the underground base. 39

Figure 5. A photo of a car that is similar to the one that visited Raechel's and Marisa's apartment. 40

Figure 6. Helen's drawing of one of the unusual-looking people she saw at a restaurant in Eureka, northern California. 55

Figure 7. Helen's sketch of the double high row of tanks containing fetuses. 112

Figure 8. Drawings of Marisa's photo frame showing its deisgn and how it defied the laws of physics. 182

Figure 9. Official college letter verifying Raechel's attendance there. 202

Preface to Volume II

*P*art II provides a summary of what was learned during the investigation. A full text transcript was made of the oftentimes emotional, traumatic, and revealing regressions. Details of the investigation, the characters, the sometimes frightening, sometimes humorous, and always puzzling events that have happened to Helen and the others connected with this investigation have been chronicled. Dr. June Steiner has documented her thoughts on this case. This information, along with one further startling event, which occurred late in the investigation, points to the ongoing nature of the Humanization Project.

An old English proverb states that, "The eyes are the windows of the soul." Raechel's eyes are the windows of humanity's soul. Looking through her eyes, we see the worst and best of humankind. Again and again, the research would reveal an answer, then the answer would reveal another secret.

Venturing to look deeper into Raechel's eyes in hopes of discovering the truth, we found ourselves unable to look away. At first Raechel's eyes were a mirror, reflecting a physical reality, our dreams, and hopes. Then she beckoned, promising more, asking us to look deeper. And again, as others had dared before, we hesitantly stepped into the world behind her eyes. We found ourselves caught behind the looking glass, at times frightened, sometimes laughing, often frustrated, and incredulous. Reality melded with unreality, normal with paranormal, revealing a new world we will never forget. In the end, we found her eyes were not just the windows to her soul; they embodied the past, present, and future of all souls.

"Read every footnote, study the appendices, check the references, no one disappears completely. Somewhere there's a trace, a forgotten fingerprint, lying hidden in the shadows, waiting to be found."
—former intelligence officer

Section 1

As Helen told her story, questions kept coming to mind. Did she really have a daughter? Had the daughter been blind? Did she attend college, and did she have a roommate named Raechel? How did she know all this stuff? Why did she know it? Was she making it up? And finally, could enough information be found to verify her story?

Today Helen is semi-retired, living off Social Security and a part-time job. She is intelligent, quiet, and somewhat shy. Never, in the years I've known her has she deviated from her story, or seemed other than a normal middle-aged mother and grand-mother.

Astounding as it sounded, I believed there was more to Helen's story and that perhaps hypnosis could help her remember.

Dr. June Steiner, a graduate of The Institute of Transpersonal Psychology and The American Institute of Hypnosis, agreed to do a regression with Helen.

Debunkers take great pleasure in extracting a sound byte from a regression, then pointing out that the hypnotherapist has, by asking what appears to be a leading question, led the person undergoing hypnosis. For example, someone reports a light in the sky. During hypnosis the hypnotist asks, "What did the UFO look like?" That's a leading question, introducing the suggestion that the object was a UFO.

It took several weeks to formulate the questions we wanted to ask Helen. Great care was taken by Dr. Steiner in allowing Helen to bring forward her experience without leading or influence by questions, tonality, or word choice, or by confirming, denying, or being surprised by what was said.

Dr. Steiner states concerning this case, "My interest in this case came when I was asked to assist in the hypnosis sessions and read Helen's story. She had extensive conscious memories, which I felt were a strong grounding for any further discoveries through hypnosis. My concern for Helen's well-being and care, and for the integrity of the inquiry, was foremost as we explored her experiences. In some instances, ideomotor responses were used to communicate directly with Helen's subconscious mind, bypassing the spoken word and conscious mind in order to obtain specific details."

Under hypnosis Helen was able to recall events that startled everyone involved, including her. We encountered deliberate suggestions by individuals and ETs to not remember or speak of events again, or of a time delay before remembering.

Dr. Steiner continues, "Many people experience screen memories, which is when they see an animal or other symbolic form rather than the ET form. This often happens because the person cannot see the actual form of the event because the mind does not believe it can be so.

"Helen saw different types of birds as screen memories and as contacts between hypnotic sessions. There were a number of unusual occurrences with pictures falling, two strange beings in a restaurant, and birds with unusual eyes. After each weekend she would experience one or more eagles that seemed to be in contact and symbolic of her experience during the sessions.

"Helen had very good recall of her experiences before the hypnosis sessions began. The sessions clarified much of that information and brought forward a great deal of additional memories. In places of fear, Helen was able to proceed and go deeper into the events and was able, eventually, to recall significant information about the relationships between her, Raechel and Marisa, and the hybrid experience. She had the capacity to recall and continue to tell her story without prodding and clearly answered questions, generally without hesitation, needing time and assurance only when the experience became unusually fearful. She also clearly substantiated earlier answers when faced with any planted questions that were occasionally used to see if she would contradict any part of her former answers."

To give the reader the full impact of what Helen experienced, a full transcript of the first regression is presented. It will establish in the reader's mind, as it did in Helen's heart, Dr. Steiner's careful and caring approach to hypnosis and hypnotherapy. It will also serve to show the difference between the television portrayals and real-life regressive hypnosis.

The investigation explored the darkest corners in the labyrinth of Helen's mind—where we saw a nice story with a happy ending slowly and inexorably metamorphose into something completely different.

Chapter 1

03/28/98:
First Regression
with Dr. June Steiner and Helen

*J*une (J):[1] (Speaking to deeper mind). In this session, going deeper, will it be all right for Helen to remember information she has not yet consciously been aware of up until this time? Good. Wonderful. And during this session between Helen and June, I want you to know that if there's anything at all that Helen needs to take care of herself, that you can signal me at any time with your fingers or she can speak at any time to let me know what she needs, whether that be bodily needs or whether it be a fear or a need to speak something else, anything at all that Helen wants, needs, or that you want or need to protect Helen in any way, simply suggest to me through your fingers, and that will be taken care of. The very first concern here is for Helen's safety and Helen's comfort, knowing that this is a session that Helen has asked for, to go deeper into her own memory, to make sense out of what has happened to her, and to find some answers so that she can help integrate along with this. Is there something that Helen would like to say at this point in time?

Helen (H):(Sobbing) No.... I have to go through with this.... I have to do it. (Sobbing)

J: It may be difficult at times....

---

1. *The hypnotic induction has been omitted.*

H: Yes....

J: You will be safe and I want you to remember at all times that you made it past this place.

H: I know....

J: You're all right. And any experiences that are uncovered are in the past and they would not be coming forward now if you were not ready to hear this information.

H: I am ready.

J: What I'd like you to do at this point in time is go back to the time when Marisa first moved out of the house to begin to attend college. I want you to go back to the apartment that Marisa moved into with a roommate named Raechel, and let yourself go back to that first meeting with Raechel, and I want your deeper mind to go over the meeting first before you speak about it, and your deeper mind will recall everything that happened during that time. Your deeper mind will catch all of the inflections of voice, coloring, sounds, intuitions, actual movement and happenings, words that were spoken. Just let your deeper mind look for all those things which you consciously have remembered and all those things which up until now have not been consciously remembered. And I'm going to count to three, and on the count of three, I want you to be at that moment just before you first meet Raechel... ready to move into the experience of meeting Raechel and all of your awareness in that time.... One, two, three... Letting yourself be there now. Tell me what you're aware of.

H: I'm saying good-bye.... to, to Marisa, and she says... I wish you could stay a little while until Raechel comes, but I don't know how... I don't know when she'll be back... and I know you have to go... and just then we hear... we hear somebody come up... up the steps. She says I think... I think that might be her. Wait a minute... and, and so it is. It is. She comes... this girl… or whatever it is, comes to the door, and I… we were standing in the doorway, and so we step back… and she comes in and… and she starts to go right by us. She's in a hurry and Marisa says, "Well wait a minute, Raechel…. This is my mother. I want you to meet her."

J: Helen, stay right where you are at this moment, and I want you to move even further into a deeper state where you are actually there and telling me what's happening in the moment—I am seeing Raechel.

H: I am seeing Raechel. I can't see her face very well… because… she has big glasses… all over her face… no, not all over her face, but her face is so small there's not much left below it… below the glasses… and… and she has… she has something on her head, a scarf… and then the scarf comes down, and it's tied underneath her chin. So I don't get a good look at her face… and she looks funny, she looks… she looks too thin, or too skinny, or… she doesn't look right. But she's in a hurry, and I can't… I don't want to stare at her but I really can't help it because she looks so funny.

J: How do you feel as you stare at her?

H: I feel awfully nervous… well, not nervous, I feel uneasy. I don't think I've seen anything like this before… she's not just a funny-looking person… she doesn't seem like a person.

J: What does she seem like?

H: I don't know… her arms are too long but I can't see them. She has long… she has a long… long sleeves on, but her arms hang down too far… or something… something isn't right… something's not right here (sobbing). But anyway I can't stare at her, that's not polite. But Marisa can't see me staring at her, so that's all right… but….

J: Just let yourself remember all the little details of what you did see. What do you remember her hands looking like?

9

H: They were too long. Her fingers were not right... they were fin-
     gers... but... they were supposed to look like fingers but... they
     looked artificial somehow... but I can't keep staring because
     she wants to go by... and... and Marisa is trying to introduce
     us and... I'm just staring... I'm not acting right... because I've
     never seen anything like this before... and I don't know what
     Raechel thinks... but I don't care really what she thinks. I'm
     so, I'm so upset... but I know I have to say I'm glad to meet
     you... and I'm not glad to meet her... I'm really not glad to
     meet her... because I'm afraid of her (sobs)... I'm afraid of
     her... (sobs)... and yet I know she's not going to do any
     harm....

J: How do you know that?

H: I feel it... and I think I'm... I think I'm overreacting or some-
     thing and I don't know what's the matter with me. Marisa's not
     afraid of her, but... but yet I think it's not so much that I'm
     afraid but I don't what this is... it's not a real person...
     (sobs)...

J: So you're picking up on something...

H: (sobs) I just feel she's... she's not right.

J: You just trust that feeling and let yourself be all right with that
     feeling that's your deeper self responding to something that you
     know and feel. What happens next?

H: Well... we get through the introductions... and she says... I...
     am... so... happy... to... meet... you... I... have... heard...
     so... much... about... you... and I think, she doesn't even
     sound right. She says, she says something nice, but... but it's...
     the whole thing is... is wrong... this is not right... she doesn't
     sound right.

J: What does she sound like?

H: She sounds like a machine... like... like a mechanical voice...
     but yet it doesn't either... it's... it's... it's how she speaks that's

so mechanical... it's not... her voice... ah... ah... I guess it was like a girl's voice... but every word was so... sounded just strange. I never heard anybody talk like that... So, anyway, I... she said that... and I said, I'm glad that I finally got to meet... No, I said I'm finally... I'm glad I finally got to see you, Raechel. And she said... I... must... hurry... which wasn't, that wasn't the right... she should have said, I'm in a hurry. I... must... hurry was not the right thing to say.

J: And as she says that, I want you to focus on her mouth and tell me how her mouth moves as she speaks.

H: I could hardly see it move. It's... it's like... when you try to talk with your, with your mouth closed or your teeth closed... like a ventriloquist.

J: Were you able to see her teeth?

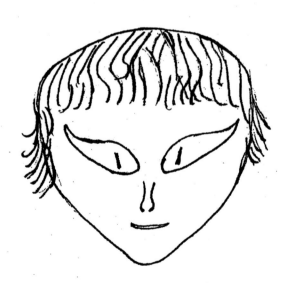

FIGURE 1. Drawing of Raechel as Helen remembers her from their initial meeting.

H: No... I didn't try to, but I don't know if 18 had any (whisper-
    ing), but her mouth was so small... and then after I said that,
    she turned and went... she went towards her room, I guess,
    and I... Marisa and I started to talk about something, and just
    then Raechel came back... we heard her come back and I
    turned... to look at her... and we had to step back and this
    time... Marisa was next to the door... and I stepped on the
    opposite side of the doorway... to give Raechel room to walk
    through... and just as she got almost to us... there was a big
    wrinkle in the rug... and just as I saw it, I wanted to... to say
    watch out... you could, you could fall on that... you could trip
    on that. And I didn't have time to say it, and then she did trip
    on it... and she couldn't catch herself... well, she didn't try...
    she didn't try to catch herself... anyone else would... would
    reach out... if there's a person on each side... you reach out to
    save yourself... you don't want to fall, so you... you grab
    whatever is there. But she didn't do that. She just... she just fell
    forward. And I reached out... because I was afraid she'd get
    hurt... afraid she'd break her glasses... I don't know why I
    thought about that... but I did. And then anyway, I grabbed
    her arm, her left arm... with both hands... and... and... she
    sort of fell halfway down but then... then I kept her from going
    the rest of the way and I helped her to stand back up... and
    when she... when I pulled her back up... her glasses fell
    down... fell forward on her nose and they... they went side-
    ways, but I didn't touch her head... I didn't... I didn't want to
    touch her head, but... but I couldn't because... because I had
    hold of her arm anyway. But her glasses slid down, and... and I
    got a look at... I looked at her eyes, and her eyes were... her
    eyes were not right... (sobbing)... her eyes weren't right... they
    were big and they were green....

J: Just keep looking at her and tell me what you see.

12

H: I was so scared for a minute... and I couldn't, I couldn't look away, I couldn't look away from her eyes... but she was more scared than I was when she looked at me... oh... I could see how frightened she was.

J: How could you tell she was frightened?

H: (whispering) She told me.

J: How did she tell you?

H: With her eyes... and I told her, it's all right, you're okay. I said that to her... and then I realized I still had hold of her arm... (crying)... and the skin wasn't right either... it wasn't right... it wasn't right... it was... it wasn't real... it... it didn't feel real. And she kept looking at me... and that time I didn't say anything. I didn't say anything.

J: What did the skin feel like? Feel it in your hands.

H: Oh... oh... it felt like mushrooms... just like cool... spongy.

J: When you say cool, how cool? Tell me, was it cold?

H: No, it wasn't... it wasn't cold. It was... I can't think... I can't think... it... it was... it... I can't think what it felt like.

J: It's all right. Just stay with the experience, and begin to tell me anything else that you are aware of about her body.

H: I should have let go of her arm, but I kept holding onto it. I... I shouldn't have touched it.

J: Why is that?

H: Because I don't think she wanted me to... But I didn't want her to get hurt.

J: I want you to go back again to the moment when you were looking into her eyes... and tell me approximately how big they were, what they looked like. Just be looking into them.

H: She didn't have any eyelids... her eyes took up the whole socket... or whatever it's called. I should know what it's called.

J: If you were comparing to a (word missing), what would be the approximate size of her eyes?

H: Uh... well... her eyes were probably the size of mine without any eyelids... the whole thing... the whole thing!... No, that's not right... (long pause)... they came up....

J: The ends came up and extended back like that?

H: Extended out like this... then they came down... the whole thing was all green... and a little thing in the middle...

J: What kind of a little thing in the middle?

H: It wasn't round. It wasn't round, it was up and down and black, and I felt as though I was just pulled into the black thing.

J: Pulled into it in what way?

H: Like that was where she told me that she was frightened.

J: So rather than be told it by a voice, it was as though you were somehow being communicated with by this black area of her eye? Is that what you're saying?

H: That's what I said.

J: Be there, looking into that black part of her eye. Tell me more about it.

H: Um... um... I can't...

J: When you say you can't, what does that mean?

H: Like she's going to see me again... that she wants to... she wants to tell me something, but she can't do it then... and I'm scared... and this is not the time for her to talk to me.

J: Well, Helen, we know that you didn't talk to her then. Would you be willing to look back in her eyes now and let her tell you what it was that she wasn't able to tell you then? You're safe, and you're here. Would you be willing to go back and re-look in her eyes and let her tell you?

H: Um... that she wants... she's supposed to be like other peo-ple... no, not like other people... she's supposed to be like peo-

ple but she can't do it. She tries... she tries to do it, and it
doesn't work out... She isn't the same. She doesn't... she
doesn't look the same... and no matter what she does... she
can't pull it off. And she's so frustrated and... and the reason
that she can get along with Marisa... is that Marisa can't see.
Not very well... so she doesn't see... Marisa doesn't see...
how different Raechel is. All she knows is that Raechel helps
her and she talks to her, and Marisa doesn't notice how
funny she sounds. She says this to me... she says, I sound
funny... and I try to talk like other... like the other people,
and I cannot do it... and she said I do not know how long I
can do this... The men tell me I have to... I do not have... I
have to do it really soon or we are giving up... they are giving up... and I try as hard as I can... but I cannot do it. And
she's really upset. And I... I don't talk to her... but I'm saying
to her... I'm looking at her... right into those slits... and I'm
telling her it's all right... it's okay... and I'm telling her, you
know you're trying too hard, and people are afraid of you,
too, and I was afraid of you, but I'm not now... and I said
you know what, your eyes are so beautiful... your eyes are so
beautiful. Because she didn't have her glasses... she didn't
have her glasses on. She took them off... but this was
another time. This was not, this was not when I first met her.

J: When was it?

H: A little later... um... I don't know. Two or three weeks... I
don't know.

J: Where did it take place?

H: In the apartment... Marisa wasn't there... I don't know
why... I don't know why I was... maybe I was waiting?... I
don't know... maybe I was waiting to see Marisa, but she
wasn't there. And that wasn't right that Raechel was there...
I don't remember how I got into the apartment. I was in the

kitchen… and I was standing by the window. She was there in the room, pretty close, four or five feet away, and she didn't have… she didn't have her scarf on either. And she was… she was really pretty.

J: What did she look like? What did her hair look like?

H: It was beautiful, red… red-blonde color. It was really thin and wispy and it was kind of… like it grew in different directions… I don't know how to explain it, but… but it was long enough… it was like it wasn't used to being combed or made to go in a direction… the right direction. It was pretty. But it was really thin and I could see why she had to wear… wanted to wear a scarf… because it didn't look quite right. But she wasn't worried about it. And I still thought it was really pretty.

J: What was she wearing?

H: Well… ah… (long pause)… it was kind of like a uniform but no, no, that's not right. It was, it was a jumpsuit… it was like a jumpsuit. But I don't know if had a top or bottom… I mean if it was separate. It… it was all one color.

J: Do you remember the color?

H: Blue… oh, a beautiful blue… like clouds, like sky-blue… and she had her sleeves rolled up… I don't know why she did that, because her arms were funny… her arms were so skinny.

J: How big around were they?

H: Oh… ah… like a little kid… like a little kid's arms… and they were so long, so long. And her hands looked… her hands looked funny, too. The fingers were just long, but they were like… like the fingers were all the same length… that's not right, either. It's not the way you should be… you're supposed to have different length… your fingers should look different. They shouldn't all look alike. But hers did. But before I looked at her arms, I looked at her face because I was looking at her eyes and thinking how beautiful, what a beautiful color they were. But then I noticed her skin, and... oh, God, that wasn't right, either. But I wasn't afraid, and I... I guess I should have been, but... but her skin was greenish, not... not bright green, but... but it wasn't pink. It's like there... there was no pink or color of a person's skin... it was greenish... and yellow... more green. And her arms were, too. I looked down then. That was when I looked at her arms first. I noticed she was the same color all over... what I could see. And then... then I noticed the fingers were... the fingers were all the same length.

J: What were the ends of her fingers like?

H: She didn't have any nails... and then, I started to feel a little sick... not very much, but I... and I tried to hide it... because I really wasn't afraid of her... but I knew she wasn't real, either... and I guess... I guess I got over that feeling because... I stayed a little longer and Marisa never did come... I don't know... I don't know how I got in the apartment.

J: I want you to go back for a moment to when you were conversing with your eyes and hers. And I want you to be looking in her eyes again, into the slits of her eyes, and tell me how long the slits were. Did they go a little ways, or top to bottom, what did they look like?

H: I never saw anything like that... I felt as if... I felt as if I was being pulled in, but... but I wasn't.

J: Let yourself be pulled in, whatever that means. Just let yourself be there. You'll be safe. And tell me everything that you're feeling, and anything that's happening. Just go into her eyes.

H: Um... (long pause)...

J: Deeper and deeper into her eyes.

H: Oh... I'm seeing lights... Oh...

J: It's all right.

H: Oh... oh, it's just like... just like... not like lightning, but it's where everything is all lit up... like flashes... Oh... but she says it's okay. She says she'll be... she's there... and it's okay, but I've never seen anything like it before... Oh... I don't feel, I don't feel that it's okay... and I tell her I... I don't want to go there... I don't want to go there... and she says no... she doesn't say it... but she tells me. Oh... and all I can see is the lights. I don't know what's happening. I don't know what is going on.

J: What color are the lights?

H: Blue and green... beautiful, beautiful shades of blue and green that I've never seen before... oh... and I don't know if I'm... I guess I'm still in the kitchen, but... but how can I be there and I can see... I can see these other things, and I feel it's like... like she wants me to go... to go wherever the lights are... but...

J: The kitchen is there.

H: The kitchen is there and I'm... and then, I am really afraid... Oh... oh, no... and then I step back and I grab the edge of the table, but I don't know why I do that... what good will that do?

J: I want you to move back a few moments before you step back and grab the table. I want you to go back to the blue and green lights, and I want you to know that the kitchen will be there when you come back out. But I want you to stay as long as you actually stayed in the presence of the blue and green lights and tell me everything that happened.

H: (Very long pause)... Oh... it's like I'm looking in a window. It's not a square window. It's longer than it is high... and there's blue light outside, but there's blue light in... there's blue light outside... and a different light in. And now Raechel's on the inside and she wants me to come through. And I tell her,

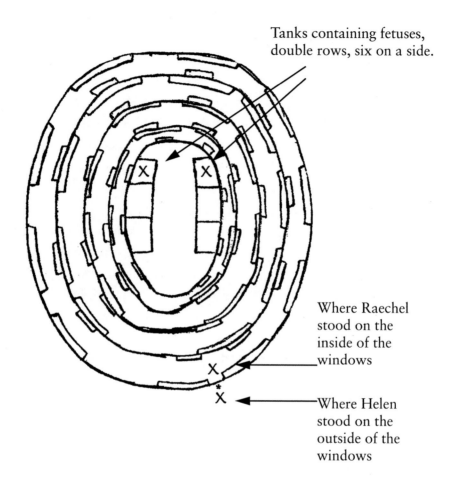

Tanks containing fetuses, double rows, six on a side.

Where Raechel stood on the inside of the windows

Where Helen stood on the outside of the windows

FIGURE 2. DRAWING OF THE PLACE RAECHEL TOOK HELEN DURING A VISIT TO THE GIRLS' APARTMENT. THE * MARKS THE SPOT WHERE RAECHEL AND HELEN TOUCHED FINGERS, ALLOWING HELEN TO PASS THROUGH THE WINDOWS AND FOLLOW RAECHEL.

(laughs) "Well, I don't see a door." She said, "There does not need to be one." She said, "Just touch the window." Oh, God... oh... and I do touch the window on the outside, and then I'm on the inside of it... Oh....

J: How did it feel going through it?

H: Oh, it was so warm and felt good... but I was so afraid... and I felt so good, too... so warm... and then... uh... and then I saw more windows... it was like it was more hallways and more windows, and I told her I can't do this. I can't do this, Raechel. I have to... she said, well this is where I am going. I just wanted to, wanted to show you. But she said, I am not going now, and she said... but I did not want you to be afraid for me when I go... And I said well, I don't know, do you just live where there's windows, or what is this place?... and she said, well, I cannot tell you now, you have to go... you have to see the whole thing. But I cannot take you there now. I just want you to... I just want to let you know that it is warm and it is beautiful. And I said I have... I have to go back... I have to take care of Marisa. I have to take care of her... and then I was back outside the windows and my hand is on the table, and I'm thinking... where was I... what happened to me... what happened to me, and Raechel is still there where she was before, and she's still... she's still looking in my eyes, but... and everything's supposed to be the same, but it isn't. Um... nothing is the same.

J: What do you mean by that?

H: I know that she came from another... another place, but I know I went there too. But I don't want to go back there.

J: Helen, I'm going to count from one to three, and on the count of three, I want you to be aware if you have ever gone back with Raechel and gone through the other hallways and windows where she lives. One, two, three!

H: (Long pause)... (whispering)... I don't think so... I don't think I've gone... I'd like to. But I never saw Raechel after that day. But I think that's where she is.

J: Has Raechel ever contacted you in any other way since that day?

H: (whispering) I think so.

J: What do you mean?

H: I've seen the eyes. Not the whole eyes, just the slits.

J: When does that happen?

H: Birds...

J: Which birds are those?

H: Oh... eagles... the eagles.

J: Where were the eagles when you saw those slits?

H: At my house... but they weren't birds.... they were more... I don't know what they were. I thought they were eagles... but... the slits were like Raechel's eyes.

J: Then just be looking at those slits, and let yourself see the eagles in any other shape or dimension they may also occur in. And just tell me what you're aware of.

H: Hm... the Christmas bird... it was my Christmas bird.

J: And what was that?

H: It's... well, that's what I call it, but I don't know what it is. That had... its eyes were like the eagles', and they were like Raechel's. But it had funny feathers. The feathers were, (laughs) they were kind of like Raechel's hair... they went funny directions, but they, they were not pretty like Raechel. They were, they were pretty for a bird, I guess. But they were red and blue, and green... that wasn't right, either... that wasn't right, but the hair... it looked like her hair. And the eyes had slits, but it made me laugh and I was so sad.

J: It made you laugh and you were so sad?

H: When I had been so sad.

J: I want you to look at your Christmas bird, into its eyes, into the slits of the eyes, and tell me what you see or feel.

H: Oh... that she was... not she... it... I don't know if it was a he or a she... the bird... uh... said that... oh, God... it was always, it would always be close to me... and I don't know if I want that. But it said there was nothing I could do about it.

J: What else did it say?

H: That I wouldn't... that I'd never see it like that again. It would never look the same... and that every time I saw it, it would be different.

J: Did it say why?

H: Um... no... no, it didn't. I don't remember if it did. But... there has to be a reason... but I'm not afraid now.

J: Good.

H: I don't always laugh like I did at the Christmas bird, but... but I feel kind of comforted when I see the birds.

J: Comforted in what way?

H: Just at peace.

FIGURE 3. A DRAWING OF THE CHRISTMAS BIRD THAT ALERTED HELEN AND AUTHOR JEAN BILODEAUX THAT SOMETHING STRANGE WAS HAPPENING.

J: And so now is it all right if the Christmas bird comes back in other forms that you may see?

H: Um, hm... it's fine. But the cats are still upset... Oh, why... why if I'm not afraid... they are really scared. But I don't care how they feel.

J: Do you think perhaps you could help them to understand in some way?

H: Oh, yes.

J: Would you be willing to do that?

H: Um, hm.

J: And now, Helen, I'd like you to go back again to when you were with the two eagles and I want you to look into their eyes and I want you to tell me what you're experiencing.

H: Oh, oh... I see those lights again. Oh, the blue lights again... Oh, oh... but I'm not going any place... I'm not going. I can't. I can't. And Sarah[1] is so afraid... oh, and I tell her... no, they won't hurt you. But she says, they will, they're so big. And I say, be quiet. They're telling me something. Oh!!! Oh... oh, (very upset)... I don't want her to leave me alone out here.

J: What just happened now? What just happened? It's all right to talk about it.

H: The whole sky was all blue flashes... and that can't be... because the sky was all gray... oh... um...

J: Let yourself be in that place. Don't compare it to anything. Just let yourself be there and tell me what you see.

H: I don't see... anything but blue lights. But I'm not... um... I'm not where I was.

H: But she was a real person... she can't be this other thing. Oh.... oh, but she is... Oh... she always was... Oh... oh...

---

1. *neighbor who witnessed the two eagles in a simultaneous sighting*

There was nothing she could do about it... there's nothing I can do about it.

J: Tell me what you know. What is it that there's nothing she can do about it?

H: She can't change where she is now. She can't change what she always was.

J: What was she always?

H: (Long pause). She wasn't always human. But she looked like it, and she acted it.... So... that's why she and Raechel... that's why... that's why... Raechel came to meet her and to meet me. Oh... why wouldn't I know? But she says I wasn't supposed to... But I thought... and I remember... Oh... oh... and she's been... she tried to... I guess she's been trying to tell me, and I didn't understand.

J: And now you have a way to communicate with them both on an ongoing basis.

H: Oh, God.... Oh (very upset)... oh, oh, oh. Ah....

J: Tell me what you just became aware of.

H: Oh, God... that I had a child that wasn't what I thought it was.

J: When was that?

H: When I looked in the eagles' eyes... that was why Raechel... that's why when I looked in... when I looked... when I looked in Raechel's eyes I thought they were so beautiful. She was, maybe she started to tell me something then. Maybe she started to tell me the truth but it wasn't... maybe she felt... oh, I don't know what she thought.

J: Perhaps you weren't ready to hear it yet.

H: I don't... I don't feel very ready right now. I think that's it. But how... how could it be?

J: Is that something you would like to investigate right now or would you like to wait a few hours or days before you'd like to do that?

H: I think I need to know now.

J: All right. Helen, I want you to go even deeper. Feel yourself floating back even deeper. I'm going to count to three, and on the count of three you are going to be in a situation where you know how this all began. Know your part in it and know why. One, two, three.

H: (Very long pause). That can't... that's not right....

J: Just let the information come through and not judge it. What is it that you're aware of?

H: Oh... hm... but... but that was too long ago.

J: How long ago was that?

H: Oh, I was too young.

J: Too young for what?

H: Too young to have a baby.

J: How young were you?

H: Um... thirteen.

J: And what happened? Tell me what's happening right now as you're there.

H: Um... well... well, I don't know how I got there, but I remember, I remember the place because I used to go there all the time.

J: What place is that?

H: It was a little place I used to go to get away from everybody, everything. Just a little place in the woods... but I... I would spend the... a lot of time there... but I don't know what I did.

J: Were you alone?

H: I don't... I would go there alone but we used to talk about... but how could I talk if I was alone?... I... something's... it was a place where I could go and I could find out things.

J: Did you hear them or just know them, or....

H: I just... I just knew them. But how can... I don't understand how I can know... how can you know things if there's... if... well, how can you learn anything from yourself? I don't... I don't... I just knew things. But no one would listen. When I would tell them, they'd say, you're crazy.

J: What kinds of things did you tell them?

H: About the light.

J: What light was that?

H: It would be a blue light... pretty, beautiful light. But they said no, no, you're just crazy. So then I didn't talk about the light any more but I still went back.

J: And when you went back and saw the light, did you stay in the place to see the light?

H: Oh, yes. It was so pretty.

J: And when you were in the midst of the light, what else happened?

H: Oh... it feels warm. Like they really... cared... really cared about me.

J: Who is they?

H: I don't know... they weren't... well, they weren't people... well, not real people... but they would talk to me.

J: What did they look like?

H: They were about the same height as I was, but they were really thin. I used to take things for them to eat, but they would never eat them. Uh... they told me they didn't like apples and things like that.

J: Did they say what they did eat?

H: No. They said their food was different. But they wouldn't show me... because I wanted to see what it was like, and they said no, it's not good for you... but your food isn't good for us, either... and so after a while I didn't bring them any little treats... but they still kept... and I don't know how they knew

I would be there because it wasn't every day. Whenever I got there they would come... but I don't know how long they stayed.

J: Did you ever go anywhere with them? Or did you always stay there?

H: I think I stayed there. They asked me to...

J: They asked you...

H: They asked if I wanted to see where they... where they lived, they said, and... I don't know, I wasn't afraid of them, so I don't know why I didn't go. But I don't think I did... But...

J: I'm going to count from one to three, Helen, and if you ever went anywhere with them to see where they lived, on the count of three you'll be there. If not, you'll be in your place. One, two, three.

H: Um... I did not go with them. But they told me I was part of them.

J: What did they tell you about that?

H: That there was nothing I could do about it... but... they would see that... it was like oversee... they would oversee... they would watch me... they would watch me... like keeping track... and that I was too young to know.

J: Did they ever tell you that you might know later, or that you might not know?

H: They didn't... it was as if I was too young then to know, but when I got older I would understand. It was as if they would not be... exactly telling me, but some other way I would know. And I was confused, I didn't know what they meant... but it didn't seem that... I didn't think of questioning them.

J: Did you ever call them by name?

H: No.

J: And did they call you by name?

H: No, I don't think so... but I... after a while I would go back and they really never came again.

J: About how old were you when they stopped coming?

H: ... Maybe another year... uh... I don't know... fourteen... no matter how many times I went back, they were never there.

J: Helen, I want you to go back to the incident that happened when you were thirteen... that you said you were too young to have happen. And on the count of three, I want you to go directly to that incident, that event, and tell me what you are aware of. One, two, three.

H: They want to know if I would like to have a baby. And I said, of course not, I'm too young... and I thought... why are you talking to me like this... and they said, oh, we just wondered. We thought you might like to have a baby. And I said, I don't want a baby now... and they said, that's all right, that's okay, you don't have to have one now... later you'll have one... later you'll have one and it'll be... different.

J: Did you ask them what that meant?

H: Yes... oh... and they said... well, it will be... a baby that will look like... it will look like you, but inside it... it will think like us... and I... I didn't know what they meant... I didn't know what they meant.

J: And now, looking back, who were they describing?

H: Marisa... but it was a long time afterwards when I had her... I don't know how that... I'm not really sure how that happened... but it makes sense... but how could they do that to me and I don't know?... Shouldn't I know?

J: Let yourself go very deep now. And let yourself request knowing how and when that happened. On the count of three, let that information come forward. One, two, three.

H: Oh.... oh....

J: What's happening, Helen?

H: Oh... I'm just... I was just having a checkup... but... but it hurts... and I haven't been sick. Oh... but that blue light is there... but... oh... I don't need a checkup. But they say it's going to be all right... I'm fine, and everything will be just fine.

J: Who is they?

H: It's a doctor.

J: What does the doctor look like? Who is it?

H: I don't know him. I should know him. But I... I don't know him. I've, I've never seen him. I've never seen anybody. But that blue light is there and it's right in my eyes. I really can't see anybody very well. But they tell me it's, the checkup was fine and I'm okay and that... that everything is... everything is all right. But that's not my doctor. I don't even have a doctor. Ah... but... how would I get there? How did I get there? I'm... I'm not... I don't even know where I am...

J: Just let yourself slowly move back a few minutes at a time until you are just before the event and tell me what you are aware of.

H: (Long pause) Um... I had to stay home tonight... had to stay home... and somebody came by to see how I was. But I wasn't sick... I saw the lady before, and she always said hello to me, but I don't know where she lives. But she's... I see her... I see her different places. She always looks at me and she always says hello, but... but I just moved there. Nobody else says hello. So why does she?

J: What does she look like?

H: People say she looks like me... but she has dark hair, so she can't look like me. And she's tall... I don't know... I don't know... but she comes... she comes to see how I am... but how would she know where I live? I live upstairs over a bakery... how could she know that? Anyway, she says that what

I need is some fresh air. And I say I'm too tired, I just want... I don't want to go any place. I don't want to go any place with her, but I can't tell her that. I don't... I don't want to say that. She said, get your coat and come for a walk. So I get my coat and we go for a walk. And we go to a part of town that I... I had seen but... I think maybe one time... as though she said I have to stop here for a minute, I have to get something. I said I'll wait. No, she said, you need to come in. So I went in... and she took off her coat, and she had on... like a green scrub suit... like in an operating room. But then I thought, well, that's okay, we're in an operating room... looks like one. It looks like a doctor, another nurse, and I guess this lady's a nurse, and I see... they had a light turned on, it was the blue... a blue light. But this was a real light. This was not flashes, this was... it was like a... a light in an operating room... overhead light. And... I don't remember... I was on the table, and that's when the doctor said... everything is fine. Your checkup is fine. And I said, I don't want a checkup, I don't need one, I'm not sick. And he said, well, it's all over, and you're fine, you'll see, you'll be okay... and so I got off the table and they put my coat on... my coat, and the lady took me home... and I don't know... I guess I went to bed... I think I went to bed. Pretty soon my husband came home.... a lot later, because he had to travel a long way to get home that night. I never mentioned it to him... because it didn't make any sense to me, and he'd just yell... it would be better he didn't know... but there was nothing I could do.

J: Do you know what year that was, Helen?

H: Um... I don't know... ah... right, it was soon after I got married, I think... ah... 1951. It had to be because... yes, that's the year I got married... but I don't know who that lady was... why would she take me... but why didn't... I shouldn't have gone. But I couldn't help it. She tricked me, because she said we were going for a walk... and then we went in that place, and then it happened.

J: What do you think happened there?

H: I think... somehow... some kind of an implant... artificial insemination... I'm sure that's what it was.

J: In the next few hours or days, you'll have a clear memory of how it happened and where it happened, and when we ask you to go back into hypnosis, you'll easily go to that place and be able to remember everything that happened. And now, do you remember seeing that same woman ever again?

H: Yes...

J: When was that?

H: Oh... oh, I know that woman now... I know her.

J: She was... she was the lady... she was the lady who... she was a doctor... but she said, she talks different now... but I went to see her because I thought I was pregnant again and I was... I thought I had a miscarriage because I was bleeding all over. And I went to see her because she was the only person I could see right away. And she didn't say very much... and she took me... she took me into... she took me into... she said she was doing a D&C. She was going to stop my bleeding. She was going to fix my problem. And that... that is the same... that is the same lady that took me for the walk. I shouldn't have gone to see her, but I didn't know she was the same woman.

J: What was her name?

H: Her first name was Rosalind. I don't remember her last name.

J: And where were you when this happened? What town?

H: Johnsonville, New York.

J: Do you remember the year?

31

H: … ah… ah… 1956 maybe… I can't remember her last name. She was a German lady. She spoke with a German accent. She was not very kind. She was really rough. I shouldn't have gone to see her. I don't know why I did.

J: Did you ever see her after that?

H: Yes.

J: For what reason?

H: She was a doctor at the hospital where I worked. So I didn't… I never talked to her. I would see her in the hallway… she was not a nice woman. Nobody liked her. So I don't know why I would go to her.

J: In the next few hours or days or weeks, you'll have a much better understanding of how you came to go to this woman for the treatment, and will be able to fully recall it at a conscious place. Is there anything else at this time that would be important for us to know about Raechel or Marisa in terms of their birth, you as a mother?

H: I don't think so. I don't know.

Chapter 2

03/28/98:
Second Regression
with Dr. June Steiner and Helen

June (J):[1] ....remember clearly everything that transpired in that meeting. And when you have that meeting clearly in mind, just raise your "yes" finger to let me know that you're there.... Now let yourself be there with the colonel, clearly aware of what's going on. And tell me exactly what's happening.

Helen (H): He's already there when I come in... and Marisa says, Raechel's father is here and he wants to meet you. And so I walk in... the living room where he's sitting on the couch, and he stands up and Marisa introduces us, but she doesn't say his first name.

J: How does she introduce you?

H: She says, this is Raechel's father... Colonel Nadien. And he stands up and reaches for my hand... and he says... I'm so glad to meet you, and... I can't remember his name, I can't remember his first name. But she didn't tell me... and I can't... it seems that he said... I'm Rich... I'm Rich Nadien... or something like that, but I didn't hear him very well and I didn't want to ask him to repeat it, but... so I guess his name would be Richard. But I'm not really sure.

---

1. *This is a subsequent regression with some missing information—blank spot in the tape.*

J: Just let your deeper mind for a moment go back in time to the other incidents where Marisa spoke to you of the colonel and used his name and just let your deeper mind swing over each conversation to see if his first name was used.

H: She always called him the colonel. And I only heard him say his name that one time, and I didn't... I really didn't get it. But I think it was Rich, so I guess it would have had to have been Richard, but I'm not sure.

J: All right, we'll just let that be fine, knowing that at any time in the next few hours or days or weeks, if a name other than Richard comes forward you'll keep it in your consciousness, will remember to write it down, and then we'll know if the name is different than Richard. For now, just let it be all right. And if during this session you should remember another name, you just bring it forward. Will that be all right?

H: Yes, that will be fine.

J: Can you tell me what it was that the colonel spoke to you about on that meeting?

H: Yes.

J: What was it?

H: He said that... since I had already probably become suspicious or had some... some doubts about Raechel's background, and I guess she had told him about... ah... the incident where I saw her face, that it was time I should know... should know the truth. And so he told me where he had... he had first seen Raechel when she was very small... and... she had looked into his eyes and he felt a bond of some sort... and she talked to him through... with her eyes and with her mind. And he didn't understand why he felt the way that he did about her because he had never felt that way about any of the other ones that he had ever seen. And... that's when he told me that he had decided to keep her and not send her back... because they needed a young one for the Project anyway.

J: What Project was that?

H: One that ATIC was... was trying to get started... no... they had started it... but for different reasons it wasn't... it wasn't working the way they had wanted it to. But with a young one, they thought maybe it would... and since he felt this special... he had a special feeling about her, that maybe that was one of the things that they had not had before, because the other ones were older and they didn't really seem to want to cooperate. But with a young one, maybe they could influence her enough so that they could learn from her and she could learn from them. So... he... he didn't know how he would do it, but he knew he would somehow or other. So when he got her back to the base... it all came together for him because everybody wanted to help. They all... I don't know why... but they all felt that they needed to do what they could. And she agreed. And then he found out... that he had to... he thought it would just be for a little while. But ATIC said no, you have to do it... you have to do it for a long time. So anyway, he went on and he told me about that... and about the problems that they'd had... they knew that they had to teach her to talk, and... she never... and she said she would try, but... but she never got very good at it, and that's why she always... she always sounded like a machine. But she was good enough so that she could pass most of the time and they helped her... he told how her appearance... they didn't know what they'd do about that... ah... it was fine on the base, but they couldn't live there forever. So, he told me about... how they had to figure out how to cover her up... so people wouldn't know what she was.

J: As he was telling you all about this, how were you feeling?

35

H: I was... I was sick inside... and yet, I was fascinated... to think such a thing could happen... and I knew he wasn't lying to me... even if he had been lying to me, I still saw her... I knew she wasn't from here. So I know he told me the truth.

J: Did he tell you any more about his job on the base?

H: When he got Raechel?

J: Um-hm.

H: Only that she was one of the few that looked halfway human. And that was another thing they looked for when they needed one that... that was closer to us... he said it was almost too much for him sometimes. He couldn't stand the sight of some of them... and, there were... lots that just didn't make it... and they tried to save them but they were burned or all broke up or something, and they couldn't do anything for them, and it wasn't the death that was so bad... it was just how these things would have looked if they had been all in one piece. So he said he welcomed Raechel coming... because he thought after the first day or so when he found that she could stay, that this was his out... so he didn't have to deal with the other stuff. But then... then he knew he had a problem because after... after a certain ... after she got so far... then he had to leave the base... and the goal was that he had to see how she would do among people. So they looked for just the right person... he didn't look, they looked... I don't know who. I didn't ask, I couldn't say anything.

J: As you watched and then listened to him talk, I want you to be very aware of his appearance, his body, his weight. Tell me everything you can remember about how he looked.

H: He was a really handsome man... and he had dark hair, dark brown... unusual blue eyes, not bright blue, but deep blue... and I don't know... I don't remember how tall he was, maybe... 5'10"... 6'... no... about that... probably about 180 pounds. He was a really well-built man. Very neat, in good shape. I didn't want to stare but he was a good-looking man.

J: About how old was he?

H: I don't know. I think he was in his early forties to middle forties... between... maybe forty-four, forty-five. I think, I don't know.

J: As you were talking with him, was Raechel there?

H: She was in her bedroom.

J: Do you know why she wasn't out talking with you?

H: She didn't want to hear it.

J: Did she say why she didn't want to hear it?

H: No.

J: I want you to focus back on the colonel again for me. As you listen to him talk, were you aware of any accents or unusual mannerisms as he talked?

H: No... he had a voice... may have been trying to have no accent... and seemed very much at ease... much more than I was... he just sat there and talked, but his voice did have no accent... and everybody has some accent, everybody should... unless you've been trained to have none.

J: And as he told you about the story concerning Raechel, is there anything he told you about what she needed to eat or how she needed to eat it, or...

H: Yes. He said she could never eat food like normal people... that's what he, like normal people do. He said he would keep her supplied with... with exactly what she should have, and he would see that it would always be there.

J: Did he say what that was?

H: Well... yes, he said, those big jugs in the kitchen on the floor, that's what she drinks.

J: Did he say what was in the jugs?

H: No, no, he didn't. It looked like water.

J: Was that liquid the only thing that she did eat?

H: No, she could... she could have the food that came in the little boxes... the little white boxes.

J: Did you ever see that food?

H: No... but Marisa told me what it looked like.

J: What did it look like?

H: She... she called it that "awful green stuff." It looked like chopped-up spinach that... that was heated, reheated too many times... and she said she had asked Raechel one time for a taste of it and Raechel told her, no, don't ever touch it. It'll make you sick. She really didn't want it anyway because it looked so awful.

J: And in this conversation with the colonel, did it take place before Raechel fell?

H: No, it took place after.

J: How long after?

H: Maybe in one or two months... not sure.

J: And how long was it after the conversation that Raechel left the apartment for good?

H: Probably another month or two... I don't remember exactly.

J: During that time, did you ever see the boxes or the jugs closely?

H: Yes.

J: Tell me what they looked like.

H: I didn't... I never touched them... but when I saw the jugs there were six of them in the kitchen and they were big like... five-gallon... like five-gallon jugs, I think. They were not small. They were like big, tall... distilled water jugs. I guess that's what they looked like and I wanted to remember... well, how could she lift those? Because they must be really heavy... but I never mentioned it because I guess it wasn't a problem... there were always six, two rows of three.

J: Were there any markings on the bottles?

H: Yes, but I didn't see them.

J: How do you know there were markings on the bottles?

H: Because Marisa, during one of the times when her sight was a little better and Raechel was gone, she checked the bottom of one and it had a triangle on it... with lines through it... and then....

J: How many lines?

H: Three. And then I saw the boxes in the freezer, and I didn't touch those, either. But they had the markings on, too. Little markings.

FIGURE 4. Triangular emblem seen on Raechel's food and water containers, on the license plate of the car driven by the men visiting Raechel at her apartment, and on a truck outside the underground base.

J: And those markings that were on the bottles and boxes, did you ever see that same marking anywhere else?

H: Yes.

J: Where is that?

H: The license plate on that funny car that those men drove.

J: Which men were those?

H: They were the men that came... they were friends of the colonel and they came... every two or three weeks to see... to see
how Raechel was doing and... and I... I saw the car one time...
and then I saw... it didn't belong to people that lived there.
Those people had old cars, and this was so strange. It didn't
look like any car I had ever been close to. I had seen pictures
like that, but there weren't any cars like that around.

J: Where had you seen pictures?

H: In old movies, or in books, history books.

J: So it was not a new car.

H: No. It looked new. It was shiny... really beautiful, but I know
it wasn't new. It wasn't American, either.

J: And that marking was on the car.

H: It was on the license plate.

FIGURE 5. A PHOTO OF A CAR THAT IS SIMILAR TO THE ONE THAT
VISITED RAECHEL'S AND MARISA'S APARTMENT.

J: Was there ever any other place that you saw that marking?

H: I don't think so. I don't remember.

J: I'm going to count from one to three and as I do, I want you to continue going deeper and deeper, looking anywhere in your awareness of ever having seen that marking anywhere else. And on the count of three, if you have any other knowledge of that marking it will come forward to you at that time. One, two, three.

H: (whispering) No, I've never seen that before. But Marisa had seen it.

J: Where had Marisa seen it?

H: She'd seen the car, too, at a different time.

J: Did she notice anything about the car that was different or more than you have already told me?

H: Not much. She knew it wasn't right, but she couldn't see it very well... somehow she knew it wasn't... it wasn't right... wasn't supposed to be there.

J: Can you tell me what else was on the license plate besides that marking?

H: Nothing. Nothing. It was black.

J: And the marking was in what color?

H: In red.

J: Was that also true of the boxes?

H: Yes... just the same, only smaller.

J: And the three men that used to bring those boxes and bottles and drove that car, what can you tell me about them?

H: I don't know if they brought the boxes and bottles. They never saw anybody... but I think they did. But they didn't bring them in the apartment, they always, whoever brought them just left them outside.

J: Outside where?

H: Outside the door. But it would be like they had just left it when the girls opened the door... the men were... funny-looking.

J: In what way?

H: They didn't look very healthy to me... they weren't thin or any-
      thing but their faces were really white... they looked... they
      just looked unhealthy like... like somebody that never got out
      in the sun, and I thought... this is California... these men...
      they don't look right for living here, but maybe they work
      inside most of the time. I didn't think much about it, except
      that they... something didn't look right, but they were mean...
      real... just... they looked like they wouldn't care if they killed
      you. That was the impression I got. And they nearly knocked
      me down the stairs as I was going up, and they were coming
      down, and there were three. Nobody stepped aside. I had to
      back down to the landing. If I hadn't of, they'd have knocked
      me down. I didn't like that.

J: I want you to be at that moment when they almost knocked
      you down, and tell me what you were feeling inside.

H: I was angry... for one thing... and I was scared. They looked
      threatening but they didn't say anything. But I knew they were
      the ones that had been coming to the apartment... I just knew.
      They were dressed so funny. They looked... their suits didn't fit
      right, and they had black suits that... they were too tight or
      something... they looked... the men looked like they had been
      dressed up to play a role or something and couldn't get suits to
      fit them right. They just did... nothing... the tops were too
      tight and they looked like they were old-fashioned or some-
      thing. They just looked out of character. They didn't... they
      looked like they should have been in the thirties or something
      and they... well, it was like they were in costume. But I guess
      they weren't because Marisa said that's how they looked the
      times that she'd seen them. So I guess that's how they always
      looked but they didn't look right. And they were rude to her,
      too.

J: As they passed you on the stairs or any other time that you might have come in contact with them, did you ever hear their voices?

H: No, I never heard them.

J: Did you ever notice anything about them in terms of perfume or smells or anything else that might be something you were aware of?

H: Perfume... they smelled musty. They smelled... they smelled like their suits had been in an old... old closet that had been locked up and things smell funny. They don't smell fresh. But they only... they went by me pretty fast, but I guess that's why I was able to smell that.

J: And was there anything else that Marisa told you or Raechel told you about these men that you don't already know from your own seeing them?

H: Um... well, Raechel... Raechel told Marisa that they wouldn't harm anyone, they wouldn't harm her. They came to check on her progress... and they were friends of her father's... they worked with her father.

J: So they worked on the base or where did they work?

H: She didn't... Marisa didn't ask. I guess... I guess they worked on the base, but maybe not... because they didn't have uniforms.

J: Did she ever call them by name?

H: No, she didn't... she didn't call them by name... but Marisa asked her the names and she told me.

J: What were their names?

H: One was Auran... and one was Asaterek... and... oh... I can't remember...I can't remember the other one. I know it, but I can't think of it.

J: It's all right, just let it be for right now. It will come back to you.

H: Oh, yes... I know it... when they talked to Marisa, they told her... they asked her to leave... one time... so she did. She didn't think she should have to leave her own apartment, but she thought it was the best thing to do... so that was the time she went downstairs and... she got a look at the car. Because by then she could see better than... than Raechel thought she could. That's when she saw the license plate.

J: Were any of these three men ever described or talked about by Raechel or her father to you?

H: No.

J: Were they ever described or talked about by Marisa as having been told by Raechel or her father?

H: I didn't understand that.

J: Did Marisa ever tell you about any one of these three men as having worked with or been with Raechel's father?

H: No. Raechel told Marisa that the men worked with her father.

J: But didn't tell you anything about any of the individual men?

H: No.

J: Is there anything else that you can remember at this time about the three men that you haven't already told me?

H: I don't remember from where I am now... but... another time I saw through a window, and one man looked like an old movie actor. It was the same man that I saw on the stairs, one of the men. He looked like George Raft. It was funny because... he doesn't look like that now, where I am.

J: What do you mean he doesn't look like that now?

H: Where I am on the stairs... that... but I saw him at a later time and I know it's the same man. And that is who he looked like.

J: How do you know it's the same man?

H: Well... maybe I don't know... but I think it was.

J: Was he with the other men?

H: No, he was by himself.

J: Where was he?

H: I was looking through a window... and he was on the other side but he didn't see me.

J: Where was the window?

H: It was just a window... I know a window has to be someplace, has to be in a wall.

J: I'm going to count from one to three. On the count of three, you're going to be at that window with the man on the other side, and you're going to know where it is that you are. One, two, three.... Tell me what you're aware of.

H: It's a car window... but he's all by himself. The other two are not there... or... I don't see the other two.

J: What kind of a car?

H: The big black one.

J: Have you ever seen this car before?

H: In the parking lot... of the apartment house.

J: And it's the same car that has the license plate with the mark on it?

H: Yes.

J: Where is this car right now?

H: (Long pause)... it's in the parking lot but in another place... but he's all by himself.

J: And what does he do when you look in the window at him?

H: He looks straight ahead but he sees me.

J: How close are you to the car?

H: Um... maybe ten... fifteen feet. But he can't see me... He's looking... he's looking in the other direction, but I think he sees me out of the corner of his eye.

J: Why do you think that?

H: I just feel it... but I don't know why he would watch... I don't know why he would be there by... himself.

J: I want you to look all around you and see if you can see the other two men anywhere.

H: No.

J: How long do you watch the man in the car?

H: Only a minute or so. Because... he's kind of scary. Because when I saw him the last time he was with the other two... and they... they just ... they tried to frighten me. And they did it. So I thought I'd better just keep walking.

J: Where were you going when you saw the man?

H: I was going up to the apartment.

J: And just continue on up to the apartment. Did anything happen between the time you left the car and got to the apartment? Did you see anybody?

H: No, I didn't see anybody but I got to the apartment and rang the bell and I guess no one was there... So I didn't have very much time to spend anyway, so I just... just came back down the stairs and left.

J: And was the car still there when you came down the stairs?

H: Yes.

J: And was the man still in the car?

H: Yes.

J: Was he still alone?

H: Yes. But I didn't see anybody else.

J: Did you ever see him or any of the other men or the car again?

H: No. I would remember that.

J: I want you to go back for a moment to when you were talking to the colonel. Let yourself go back, be in front of him, fully aware. And I want you to tell me if you ever saw the colonel again after this meeting.

H: I don't think so. I never saw him there. I don't think I ever saw him anyplace else.

J: When you spoke directly to Raechel at the time that you described to me when she told you about herself, when you saw her eyes clearly, and you looked at her hair, did she tell you anything new about the colonel that you didn't already know?

H: No....

J: Did she tell you how she felt about the colonel?

H: She loved him... and I didn't know what she meant because... I wondered if they knew what love was.

J: Why did you wonder that?

H: Because I knew she wasn't from here... But she said... she was supposed to learn to feel like we do. So I guess she could learn.

J: What kind of behavior did she display to Marisa?

H: Did Raechel display?

J: Um-hm.

H: Friends... not in the sense that other girlfriends do...

J: One, two three.

H: ...that it was difficult at all for Raechel... I don't know why I said that.

J: As you were talking through eye contact with Raechel, did she ever describe this place where she was when she was finished developing?

H: No.

J: Did she ever at any time talk about what it was like where she lived?

H: (long pause)... nothing except... that it didn't matter if... like here, it mattered if you looked different, or if you were different in any way. But there, they all look the same, so... so you didn't have that problem.

J: Did she ever talk about what it looked like where she lived?

H: Just the colors.

J: What colors were those?

H: Blue... green.

J: When she talked about those colors, how did she describe them?

H: She made me see them... she didn't make me... she let me see them... and they're beautiful. I don't know what they were... if they were... if they were sky or water... when I looked they didn't seem to be... they were just colors.

J: Did she ever mention to you family or who might have taken care of her when she was in this place before she came to Earth?

H: No... she didn't... there didn't seem to be any family. Not like a mother and father... because there wasn't a mother and father... I don't think there were any brothers and sisters, either. But I don't know that... there was no mother and father, but I don't know about the brothers and sisters.

J: Did she ever tell you how she happened to be in that ship that arrived in the desert?

H: She was supposed to be here... the other hybrid was already here... and she was supposed to come... everything was ready for her. And she didn't have any choice, she had to come... (whispering)... she had to come.

J: Did she know why she was coming?

H: Not really. But then she had no choice. She had to do what she was told.

J: How did she feel about that?

H: She didn't have any feelings. But... they just told her that it was time for her to go... and she couldn't question it... It didn't matter... she didn't have any feelings... not then.

J: What do you mean, not then?

H: Because after she came... she began... she was supposed to... the Project didn't work out with the older people... they couldn't... they couldn't fit in because... it wasn't feelings, it was... it was like love, hate, emotions. And the older people couldn't... they just couldn't seem to... they didn't work out. The Project thought that maybe... maybe if they tried with a younger one, that maybe it would, maybe they could be taught, maybe they could learn.

J: And when she first landed here in the crash landing, did she tell you what that was like for her?

H: Not much... not much... except that... that she was sort of trapped... and she thought maybe no one would find her, and she couldn't get out. So then, when someone did find her, he could talk to her... he did talk to her.

J: How did he talk to her?

H: With his eyes.

J: He knew how to speak the way she spoke?

H: That's right. Because he had spoken before... with other ones... and so... he took her out and gave her... took her... took her to a safe place. And then he told her that she could stay.

J: And did he tell her his name?

H: Not right then... not very long, though.

J: As they got to know each other better, did she ever tell you what she called him?

H: She called him by his first name... but I don't remember... she didn't call him father... anything like that... I don't remember what... I don't remember what, but it was his first name... oh... I should remember that.

J: Helen, I'm going to ask your deeper mind to answer me with your fingers for a moment. Just let yourself go totally into that place where your deeper mind will answer my questions. Was Helen ever told the colonel's first name by Raechel?

H: She didn't tell me. I don't know why she didn't... um... but she didn't call him father... but he wasn't her father.

J: I'd like the deeper mind to answer again and Helen can just allow her fingers to answer the questions. Did Helen ever hear the colonel's first name from anyone?

H: Don't know if yes or no. (fingers)

J: Did Helen ever hear the colonel addressed by some other name other than "the colonel" and his last name?

H: Don't know if yes or no. (fingers)

J: Is there any other information about the colonel that Raechel told you or Marisa that you are not allowed to speak at this time?

H: Yes. (fingers)

J: Yes. Is this information that you will allow yourself to remember and speak in the following weeks or months?

H: Not sure if yes or no. (fingers)

J: Was there some kind of condition or threat or some other way that you were told not to reveal this information?

H: Yes. (fingers)

J: Allow yourself to relax and go twice as deep as you are now. And if we come to a place where you're not allowed to let that information come out, then I want you to lift your middle finger so that I'll know that you're not allowed to answer that question at this time. Did the colonel ever mention any previous duty stations where he served?

H: No. (fingers)

J: Was there any other part of his life that he did talk about?

H: No. (fingers)

J: And now I'd like the deeper mind to allow Helen to speak.

H: The colonel didn't talk to me about those things.

J: Did he talk to someone else about those things.

H: Yes.

J: Who did he speak to?

H: Marisa.

J: Can you tell me what it was he told Marisa?

H: (long pause)... he told her about where he'd been before Nevada.

J: Where was that?

H: Nebraska.

J: Did he tell her where he grew up?

H: Yes.

J: Where was that?

H: Idaho.

J: Did he say where in Idaho?

H: Nampa.

J: Did he ever tell her the school that he attended?

H: Not the name... just... he went to school there... to high school and graduated.

J: And when did he leave there?

H: Right after high school.

J: And where did he go directly after high school?

H: Texas.

J: What happened in Texas?

H: He went... he went through training... like everybody else.

J: And when he finished that training?

H: Got a different place to go... but nobody would tell him where it was... and no matter who he asked, no one would tell him. They just said it was a mistake. But he knew it was not a mistake. But before he could go there, he... he had to go to Nebraska.

J: Do you know where in Nebraska?

H: He had to go to special school, and... it was at a big base... a big Air Force base.

J: Do you know the name of that base?

51

H: Crawford was the name.

J: And what kind of training did he have there?

H: It was a different school... different school than he'd ever seen, ever been in... all they learned about... was... other places. Spaceships... but all the other people in the class... they were all going to different places... different bases and they were all... nobody knew why they were there. They were just all sent... just all sent.

J: Was there anything that all of these people had in common?

H: Well, they had... they were all like outcasts from their families... didn't have any families... no wives, no girlfriends... maybe orphans... they were all different, but different reasons, but they were all the same, too... and... the colonel had a father and mother but they didn't want him... and he really didn't have any friends, either, any more.

J: Why is that?

H: Because he was different... everybody else just stayed home. He went away, and when he came back... they didn't bother about him...

J: While he was at these bases, what kind of security clearance was he given?

H: He had Top Secret and Crypto first... which he shouldn't have had.

J: Why is that?

H: Didn't need it then, while he was in basic.

J: So he was given that right away...

H: After two or three weeks. He shouldn't have gotten any clearance in two or three weeks, because it takes longer.

J: Was he given higher clearances or other clearances?

H: Before he went to Nebraska... just before he went to Nebraska, it was changed... and then... and then it was MAJIC... and nobody told him what that was because every-

body said they didn't know, they never heard. But he knew
that wasn't... that wasn't true.

J: What wasn't true?

H: That they didn't know. They didn't talk about it.

J: How did he feel about getting all this clearance and all of the
information he was beginning to learn?

H: He didn't really know how to handle it... it seemed too
much, it happened too fast. But he wanted to know more...
and then... he found out he was going to a different place
than the others. He was the only one... the only one that
would go there.

J: And where was that?

H: It didn't even have a real name... it was called Four Corners... and they wouldn't tell him where that was, either. But
by then, he was used to nobody telling him anything, so he
just... just went along with it.

J: And when he got there, what did he find?

H: Four Corners?

J: Yes.

H: Not much. He thought he was in the wrong place, but he
wasn't. He was... he thought there would be like a regular
base, but... but all there was was old... funny old build-
ings... just, just old barns and things... on top of the ground.

J: Was there something else there?

H: Oh, yes. Oh, yes. Underground was the whole thing. Everything. That was just a cover-up... it was just to fool people.

J: Tell me more about what was underneath the ground.

H: Places to live... laboratories... big ones.

J: What did they do in the laboratories?

H: (long pause)... worked on different kinds of... things that
made... like... things that made the ships run... things they
got from the ones that they brought in that crashed... they

take them apart... what was left... try to figure out... figure out how to... how the things worked... But he didn't go there very much because he didn't understand that.

J: What was his job?

H: His job was to go out and pick up the stuff... the people, but they're not people... the pilots... not pilots, either... the things that drove the ships.

J: What do you mean, things?

H: Well, he didn't know what else to call them... some weren't... weren't very easy to describe... and then some... some were like Raechel. But not very many of those lived... At first he didn't know why... why those ships could go so far and they'd crash when they got here... then he found out they were being shot down... in other places.

J: Who was shooting them down?

H: We were... he couldn't question very much.

J: When you said some of the occupants of these ships were very different, what did they look like?

H: (long pause)... like bugs, some did...

J: Can you tell me what kind of bugs?

H: Like grasshoppers... some of them. That can't be, but... but it was... it made him really upset... but it was his job so he had to do it.

J: And was he able to communicate with each of these that lived?

H: Most of them... the ones that wanted to, but some didn't want to... and he tried, but... then he couldn't with those, but most of them he could... he didn't know how... he didn't know why he was so good at that.

(Tape change--small amount of session is missing)

H: ...members of the team who went with him, but they weren't even going to look inside. They were just going to let it go.

J: How did he know to look inside?

H: He felt... he felt somebody was in there... something... because he couldn't see, he just felt there was something there.

J: Helen, have you or any of the people you know seen any of those buglike creatures since the time Raechel came into your life?

H: (long pause)... I don't know.

J: I'm going to count from one to three, and as I do, let yourself and your deeper mind look fully over the time period between when Raechel came and now. One, two, three.

H: Oh... oh... not... they didn't look like bugs, but their faces weren't really human.

J: Tell me what they looked like.

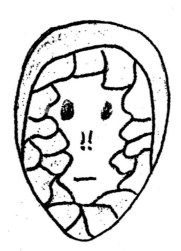

FIGURE 6. HELEN'S DRAWING OF ONE OF THE UNUSUAL-LOOKING PEOPLE SHE SAW AT A RESTAURANT IN EUREKA, NORTHERN CALIFORNIA.

H: Um... they were... like they had layers of... like they had patches ... sewed on top of patches... but they weren't green... like bugs are... but... oh... I don't know.

J: Where did you see them?

H: In... when I was in a restaurant... they didn't look like bugs but their faces weren't real... they weren't the right color for people, either, but... they weren't... they weren't green.

J: What color were they?

H: Brown, not dark brown... kind of different shades of brown... but it was like patches... all over, and they both looked alike.

J: And did you communicate with them in any way, or they with you?

H: Oh, I think so... I think so.

J: What do you mean?

H: Well, they looked at me... through the window... really close.

J: What were you aware of as they looked at you?

H: That they'd been looking for me and that... they couldn't find me ... before... but why would they want me?

J: Allow yourself to look at them now, very closely, and to look at their eyes and ask them, why were you looking for me?

H: They wanted to make sure I was safe... what could they do?... what difference would it make?... what could they do?

J: Ask them why they were interested in seeing if you were safe. What connection do they have with you?

H: Oh... I don't want to be connected with them... they look bad.

J: But they wanted you to be safe.

H: Yes.

J: Ask them why they were interested in keeping you safe.

H: Because they know I was so upset... and they were afraid... and they don't know anything about cars, and they thought I would... they thought it was too big a trip for me to take... that's ridiculous... that's stupid.

J: Why were you upset?

H: Ah... ah... because I was so late getting started on the trip and it's a long... it's a long drive... and I wanted to start early and I couldn't because I couldn't... I tried to help the boys find each other... because they were coming up together... the one had come so far already from San Diego and he couldn't find the other one... no one would answer the phone in the house... no one would answer when I called. I couldn't wait any longer... and I knew I had to get there in time to go to the cemetery.

J: Why were you going to the cemetery?

H: (crying)... I had to go see Marisa. The cemetery was going to close... and I got lost, I took the wrong street, had to ask directions and nobody knew. Finally I saw a man coming along and he told me where it was, and then I had to leave. I couldn't stay very long because they were getting ready to close it up, close the gates... and I was upset over that. And I was so hungry, I hadn't eaten all day.

J: While you were there with Marisa, were you aware of anything at all between the two of you?

H: Just something she used to say... "whatever it takes, mom, you can do it"... it didn't... I don't know what she meant... she said, you'll do all right, you'll be okay... I said I don't want to have to hurry, I can't come back in the morning, I don't have time. I want to be here ... and she said, it's all right, I'm not really here anyway... so I had to go... and I was upset. Because nothing... the whole day was awful. And when I went to the restaurant I was so thirsty and all I wanted was a nice, cold beer and the waitress brought me a warm one, and I was so mad. And I yelled at her... I said I won't pay for this, bring me a cold one... if you don't have cold beer, I want some cold water ... this is ridiculous... so I got the cold beer and ordered my supper, and just as she brought it, I looked out the window... oh... I thought ... I don't need this... I just... I can't handle this... I saw these two people, these two things, and I don't even want to look at them. But I thought, well, don't look... they'll be out of sight... don't look at them. But they weren't out of sight. They came right down... down the street, right by the window where I was, and they stopped and they looked... they just looked at me...

J: I want you to look at them very closely and I want you to tell me if you've ever had contact with these two people or creatures, whatever they are, before, in any form.

H: The eyes are all the same... all the eyes are the same.

J: What do you mean?

H: All these things have the same eyes... they all look different but... the rest of them... but their eyes are all the same... ah...

J: Like Raechel's eyes?

H: These are just big black eyes...

J: When you say they're all the same, who else has eyes like this?

H: The birds... (long pause)...

J: Is there anyone else?

H: (whispers)... the doctor... Oh... oh... (sobbing)... I don't know (can't understand)... can't get away... no matter where I go... but the other ones don't hurt me....

J: Is the doctor the only one that's ever hurt you?

H: Yes.

J: Did the doctor ever examine you or do anything at all with your body other than that time that you have described to us where she took you into her office?

H: No... I don't remember anything. So I don't know why she did it then. Well, I guess she did it because I went to her, but I don't know why I went. I should have gone someplace else.

J: When you speak, Helen, of all of the rest of them having the same eyes, do they all feel as though they are connected in some way?

H: I don't know... sometimes they look so strange that I'm really afraid. I'm startled because some of the birds don't look right... they're fierce... they've fierce eyes but they don't... they don't mean me any harm. But they look fierce... but that's how birds' eyes look. They can't help how their eyes look.

J: Helen, I'd like you to go back now to when Raechel first arrived on the ship when the colonel found her, and tell me the name of the project that she came to work with and that the colonel was working on.

H: It was the Humanization Project.

J: The Humanization Project?

H: Supposed to see how human... but I don't know... how much emotion they could develop... in... in the hybrids... they didn't... it didn't work... on anybody but the hybrids.

J: It didn't work with just the ETs?

H: That's right. They tried and it... I don't know... it just didn't work.

J: Is this what the colonel told Marisa?

H: Yes.

J: Where was the safe place they took Raechel to?

H: What safe place?

J: After Raechel was brought here and cared for and taught. How was she kept safe as they went out into the world?

H: On the base. They made a place for her to live, but somebody was always there.

J: Who was there?

H: There were two... two nurses.

J: What were their names?

H: I don't know... I don't know... but one was always with her.

J: Did Marisa ever tell you the names of the nurses?

H: No, I don't think she knew... maybe she did.

J: Did Raechel ever tell you about the nurses?

H: She didn't call them nurses.

J: What did she call them?

H: She just called them females... they had names but I don't know what they were.

J: And who began to teach Raechel?

H: A lady from the Project.

J: The Humanization Project?

H: Um-hm.

J: And what was it that she taught Raechel?

H: How to speak... how to put her thoughts into words... because she had to learn... she had to learn for the Project.

J: Was there anyone else who was a hybrid that could speak? Had this been done before?

H: Yes. There was another hybrid there. He was working on something else. He was... he was working on something else but he helped Raechel because they were... they were really alike... close... so... he made something for her to eat and to drink... and he knew how to do it because before... when they had the ETs... they couldn't keep them alive. There was nothing... it wasn't right what they gave them to eat and drink... so he made... he made his own things and it was the same for Raechel. It would work with Raechel. And he helped... he helped her learn to speak.

J: Do you know if Raechel ever saw him again after she left the base?

H: I don't know. I don't think she did but I don't know.

J: Helen, I want you to go back in time a short ways, and I want you to tell me about anything you know concerning the training in Texas and where in Texas it was that the colonel went.

H: Oh... it was where they all go to... Lakeland... Lakeland Air Force Base... think it's... I think it's near San Antonio... No... Wichita Falls, maybe... I don't know... it's one or the other... I've never been there.

J: And did you ever visit the area around Four Corners?

H: I think so.

J: When was that?

H: I don't know.

J: Was it before or after you met Raechel?

H: I never heard of it before... so... so it would... I don't remember. I don't know how I would go.

J: Were you ever at the base at the Four Corners?

H: (long pause)... I must have been... because I know what it looks like... but... but I don't know how I would go there... why I would go there... I don't know... I don't think... but if I didn't go, then I wouldn't know what it looked like...

J: Let your deeper mind take over for a moment. Let your deeper mind recall how you found out about what the base looked like. Let your deeper mind clearly look at all the information surrounding your knowledge of the base, and then let your deeper mind answer with your fingers as to what happened to allow you to know more about the base. Did Helen ever visit the base at Four Corners?

H: Yes.

J: And when Helen visited the base at Four Corners, was it after Raechel and the colonel left the base?

H: Yes. (fingers)

J: And did Helen go with the colonel and Raechel to the base?

H: Yes. (fingers)

J: And was it during the time that Raechel and Marisa lived together?

H: Yes. (fingers)

J: And did Helen go only once to the base?

H: Yes. (fingers)

J: And while Helen was there, was she taken to the base underneath the ground as well as above?

H: Yes. (fingers)

J: Was Helen at that time told anything about whether she could speak about this again or not?

H: Yes. (fingers)

J: Is it all right for Helen to tell us at this time what she was told about not speaking?

H: No. (fingers)

J: Was there a threat made of any kind?

H: Yes. (fingers)

J: Was there a threat of harm made to Helen's life?

H: Yes. (fingers)

J: Was there a threat made to anyone else's life?

H: Yes. (fingers)

J: Was there a threat made to Marisa's life?

H: Yes. (fingers)

J: To the colonel's life?

H: Yes. (fingers)

J: To Raechel's life?

H: Yes. (fingers)

J: To anyone else's life?

H: Yes. (fingers)

J: Do we know the other person or persons who were threatened with their lives?

H: Yes. (fingers)

J: Can Helen tell us who they are?

H: Yes.

J: Helen, who were the other people who were threatened with their lives if they spoke about your visit to the base?

H: My boys... so I can't tell (whispering).

J: When or if it is ever safe for you to give forward that information, it will be easily accessible to you. Until that time it is important that you do whatever you need to do to protect your family and yourself... Can you tell us any more about the surrounding areas of the base now so that we have a better understanding where it's located?... Where would that be?... What is it that you're aware of?

H: It's... it's just... it's hard to describe it because I know what it looks like, but... if I was there I would know where... where to turn... but it's really hard to tell somebody else because it's all desert there.

J: If you saw a map with roads on it would you be able to say where it is?

H: I already have.

J: You already have a map or you already have seen a map?

H: I've already seen a map and I've already done that.

J: And who have you told or shown?

H: Jean, some of the others.

J: So that they know enough how to get to the base?

H: That's right... they could find it okay.

J: Did the colonel ever mention to you or did Raechel ever tell Marisa or you any other organizations that he was affiliated with outside of the Humanization Project and MAJIC?

H: NRO.

J: What is NRO?

H: National Reconnaissance Organization.

J: And do you know what he did with that organization?

H: They were... they were like his boss or something... but... but about the same as ATIC. They all worked together... but nobody knew about anything... nobody outside knew... there wasn't any such thing... that's what they told everybody, but that's not true... just not true.

J: Do you know anything else about those connections that would be helpful for us in our looking for the colonel?

H: Um... no... I tried but I can't think... don't know.

J: Helen, I want to go again to your deeper mind and I want your deeper mind to answer some questions. Let your deeper mind move your fingers. Have you been contacted in any way by the colonel since the colonel and Raechel disappeared and moved from the apartment?

H: No. (fingers)

J: Have you received any information from any other source telling you about them?

H: No. (fingers)

J: In your visits from the birds and their invitation to look in their eyes and to go and visit that other place, have you ever been given specific information about that other place?

H: Yes. (fingers)

J: And deeper mind, Helen has mentioned to us a number of times the term "window." She has seen the man dressed in black in the car that delivered the food through the window. She again saw him looking like George Raft at the same time she saw the symbol that was on the food cartons and on the license plate, upside down, through a window. She saw the two strange beings with the patches on their faces through the window. Is there is a special significance in the term "window" for Helen when she speaks about that?

H: Yes. (fingers)

J: Is Helen free to know at this time the meaning of "window"?

H: No. (fingers)

J: Does Helen know about the meaning of "window" but it's not all right to tell it at this time?

H: Yes. (fingers)

J: Will Helen be allowed to talk about or be aware of what the window means in the next few months?

H: Yes. (fingers)

J: And will she be able to allow this information to come up naturally into her own consciousness?

H: (fingers. The answer is not to be told at this time - June)

J: Would someone else be able to assist Helen in finding out the meaning of the window?

H: Yes. (fingers)

J: Helen is raising her middle finger. Deeper mind, are you trying to tell us that there is some issue with her being helped to find out the meaning of "window"?

H: Yes. (fingers)

J: I want to assure the deeper mind and Helen that that information will not be taken or forced until Helen is ready to release that information, until it's safe, until she feels safe internally. It is important that Helen and the deeper mind know that that will not be forced before it's the correct time... I would like to ask one last question about the windows, if it's all right... Are the windows a way of alerting Helen in some way to the fact that the experiencing is continuing?

H: Yes. (fingers)

J: I'd like to ask the deeper mind if Helen was contacted or involved in any way with ET experiences before the age of five.

H: No. (fingers)

J: Before the age of ten.

03/29/98:
Third Regression
with Dr. June Steiner and Helen

June (J):[1] How was it moving?

Helen (H): It was just kind of... skips along... skips along but it's not on the ground, either... and... it stops a little way away from me.

J: And how are you feeling while this is happening?

H: I can't take my eyes off it.

J: What color is the light?

H: Blue... really beautiful blue... like the sky.

J: And then what happens?

H: I want to touch it... but something tells me not to.

J: Are you close enough to touch it?

H: I'm close enough and I reach out, but just before I do... before my hand is on it... I get a feeling I shouldn't.

J: Why shouldn't you?

H: Because I might go inside it.

J: How would you do that?

H: I don't know... and I don't... I'd like to touch it, but I don't want to go inside it... because I don't know what's in there.

J: And then what happens next?

H: It's like I'm told... that's okay... we just wanted to... we just wanted to come and see you today... but we'll be back

---

1. *The induction has been omitted.*

another... we'll be back again... we don't want you to touch us today... and I'm thinking, this is... this is silly... a light is talking to me... but it seems to be okay... so it doesn't do anything more... it sits there for a minute... and it skips along... back... backwards a little bit... and I think, well, I should have... I should be saying something to it, something more... and then I... and then it just goes away... it just goes away... but I can't tell anybody... can't tell anybody about it.

J: Why is that?

H: Because I was told not to.

J: Who told you that?

H: Just how I felt from the light... because there wasn't anybody... wasn't anybody in the light... but I hope it will come back.

J: Helen, I want you to go forward in time to the next time the light returns. Tell me where you are and what you're aware of.

H: I'm in the same place because I like to go there because I'm alone... I look up on the bank in front of the trees, and the light is there again... (long pause)... and this is when they... this is when they ask me, would you like to have a baby? (Laughs)... and I said, I don't want a baby, I'm just a little girl. Don't want a baby... I have to go to school.

J: And did you go into the ship this time? Did you reach out and touch the ship and go inside?

H: I didn't go inside.

J: What did you do?

H: I touched it.

J: And what happened when you touched it?

H: It felt like... I felt like an electric shock... and I couldn't take my finger right away... I couldn't take it away as quick as I wanted to... it's like it was stuck there for a minute.

J: What happened during that minute, Helen? Let yourself know everything that happened during that minute.

H: But I still didn't want to have a baby. I was too young. And they said, that's all right, we'll wait, we'll wait... and I don't remember... my finger came off it... and I was just standing there with my finger out, and the light was gone... I thought maybe I imagined it, but I don't think I did.

J: Helen, I'd like to talk to your deeper mind for a moment and let it answer with finger signals. I'd like you to go with your deeper mind to that moment that you touched the ship, the light, whatever it was, and in that instant I want you to tell me if something happened that you do not consciously recall.

H: Yes. (fingers)

J: Would you be willing to let that come to your consciousness at this time?

H: No. (fingers)

J: Is that something that you would be willing to allow to come to your consciousness within the next few months?

H: You don't know or you're not sure whether it's all right. (fingers)

J: Is it all right if we check back with you in the near future?

H: Yes. (fingers)

J: Can you tell me, Helen, if whatever it is that happened during that minute that you touched the light, was it longer than one minute of our time?

H: Yes. (fingers)

J: And did you have an experience different from any other experience you'd had before then?

H: Yes. (fingers)

J: Thank the deeper mind for answering those questions. I'd like to go back for a moment to your birth with Marisa, and tell me if there was... actually tell me what happened when Marisa was born. Tell me about the birth and about the conditions.

H: She was so little... she was so small... I felt so bad because I couldn't take her home with me.

J: How much did she weigh?

H: Four pounds and ten ounces.

J: Was she a healthy baby?

H: Yes, but she wouldn't eat very much. But she was healthy.

J: Was she full-term?

H: No.

J: How old was she?

H: I think eight months... I wasn't very healthy when I... before I had her... couldn't eat a lot of things.

J: Did that happen just during the pregnancy?

H: Yes... and it's happening now, too, sometimes.

J: Tell me more about that. What is it that happens? And what are those things that you can't eat?

H: I can't eat very much meat... sometimes I can't eat anything.

J: What happens if you do?

H: I feel really sick, nauseated... just like I did then... then sometimes I'm okay, but... it's new, now... it's just the last few months. I don't know why... I like to eat, but... food just looks awful sometimes.

J: When you first held Marisa, how did that feel?

H: (long pause)... not like I know it should have.

J: What do you mean?

H: I didn't feel like a mother... like a mother should.

J: Was Marisa your first child?

H: Yes... I didn't know how to feel... I guess she was so little I was afraid I'd break her.

J: And how long did it take you to bond with her?

H: A long time... it shouldn't take that long.

J: How long was that?

H: Years.

J: What finally created the bond?

H: I don't know... I think it was when she lost... no... she had gotten diabetes. She was so sick I thought she would die... it's awful.

J: What was awful?

H: It took so long.

J: But somehow there was a stronger connection when she got diabetes.

H: Yes... and why would that be?....

J: During that time before the birth of Marisa, and those years when she came down with diabetes, do you ever remember being visited by the blue light?

H: No... no, I don't.

J: And during the time when Marisa came down with diabetes, and you first met Raechel, do you remember being visited by the blue light?

H: No... no, I don't.

J: I'm going to ask your deeper mind for a moment to answer some questions with your fingers. Deeper mind, I'd like you to review Helen's life fully in the time just before Marisa was conceived to the time that you and Marisa met Raechel. Was there any contact of any kind between entities from another place and Helen—in any form?

H: Yes. (fingers)

J: Did that take place before the conception of Marisa or at the conception of Marisa?

H: Yes. (fingers)

J: Was it repeated again after Marisa was conceived?

H: Yes. (fingers)

J: Were they in contact after Marisa came down with diabetes until you met Raechel?

H: No. (fingers)

J: Were you contacted more than five times between the conception of Marisa and the time she came down with diabetes?

H: No. (fingers)

J: Were you contacted more than three times?

H: No. (fingers)

J: Were you contacted two times or less?

H: Yes. (fingers)

J: Were you contacted two times?

H: Not sure of response. (fingers)

J: Were you contacted any other time besides around conception? Between conception and when Marisa came down with diabetes?

H: Not sure of response. (fingers)

J: Was there any connection between that contact and Marisa's illness?

H: Not able to tell me at this time. (fingers)

J: Was Marisa in any way altered—was the egg or sperm that came to form Marisa in any way altered from its original form?

H: Yes. (fingers)

J: Are you able to go to that time when you were told or shown about that alteration?

H: Yes. (fingers)

J: I'm going to count from one to three...

H: One night... and I'm there by myself... and she says, it's so nice out, let's go take a walk. And I say, I don't even know who you are. And she said, that's all right, we'll get acquainted... I said, I don't want to go... and she says, well, come on anyway... and so I went... I shouldn't have but I did. I know now I shouldn't have gone... but it was such a little... such a little town and it was still light out, and I thought I... I went with her.

J: And you had seen this woman before, or you'd never seen her before?

H: I had seen her before... met her on the street.

J: What did she look like?

H: Nothing outstanding... uh... dark hair... I felt as if I knew her somehow, but I knew I couldn't... I don't think I did... because I had just moved to that town, so... and I had never been there before, so I couldn't... couldn't have known her there... So anyway we went for the walk...

J: What happened while you were on the walk? Did you talk?

H: Oh, yes... but I don't remember what we talked about...

J: Where did you go?

H: We had to stop to see somebody she knew... (long pause)...

J: Tell me about that.

H: Well, we went in, but it was somebody that wanted to see me....

J: What did this person look like?

H: Like a doctor.

J: Was it a woman or a man?

H: It was a woman and I don't like woman doctors.

J: Why don't you like woman doctors?

H: Because they always hurt.

J: Why did this doctor want to see you?

H: I don't know... but she said she needed to see me. She needed to make sure... make sure I was all right... I told her, I am all right... I don't need you to tell me that. But she said, well, you're here, so I will look anyway... I will make sure you're all right... so I lay... I sat up on the table... I didn't want to lie down.

J: What kind of a table was it?

H: It was like an exam table, examination table.

J: What was it made out of?

H: It was like it was covered with a brown plastic or something. It was an old-fashioned thing... it was an old-fashioned room... it was... but I didn't know there was a doctor's office there... ah... I shouldn't have gone with this lady. I should have stayed in the house, but... but I am... I'm here.

J: And what happened during the examination?

H: They made me lie down... and then they turned the light on and I couldn't see. I had to close my eyes, but then... then I don't remember... I don't remember... it's like... it's like... they gave me some anesthesia or something, but I don't remember the smell because... because ether smells funny and so does that thing on your face... I didn't smell that.

J: How did they give you what they gave you? What form?

H: It was in the light, I think... because as soon as I lay down, the light was so bright I had to close my eyes, and I don't remember anything, but the light doesn't do that... but there wasn't anything else either... but I don't remember what happened.

J: Was the woman who brought you to this place in the room?

H: Yes.

J: Was there anyone else in the room?

H: The doctor, the lady doctor.

J: Anyone else?

H: I didn't see anyone else.

J: And what instruments or furniture or anything else might have been in the room?

H: There wasn't much in there. There was this table that I was on, and a light up above... from the ceiling... and an old cabinet with two doors... two glass doors... really old... I didn't see... I don't remember anything else. It didn't have enough things in it. It should have had more.

J: Helen, I want you to go to the moment they turned the light on. I want you to be looking up into the light. I want you to be aware of what it felt like and what you saw. Be fully in the experience and tell me what you're aware of.

H: I could see the color of the light even... even though my eyes were closed... and it was so warm... it just really felt good all over, all around me, even though I didn't want to be there... and all I could see was just blue... it was blue... and really warm... but my eyes were closed, so I guess I didn't see blue... I didn't see anything, but I had the impression that I did...

J: And how long were you on the table?

H: I don't know. I didn't have a watch... I didn't... I don't know if there was a clock... I didn't look... maybe... I don't really know... maybe ten minutes... fifteen.

J: What time was it when you started your walk?

H: About 5:30 or 6, at night... it was still daylight.

J: And when you came out from seeing the doctor, was it still light?

H: No... it wasn't very dark, it wasn't really dark... but the sun was not out.

J: What time of the year was it?

H: Spring... early. Maybe it was... 8 o'clock. I don't really know, but by the time I got home it was dark... I didn't live very far away.

J: Did you go home with the woman?

H: She walked me home. And we went straight home.

J: And how did your body feel as you went home?

H: It hurt.

J: Where did it hurt?

H: Really deep inside it hurt... it felt... I don't know how to say it... it felt like... there was something there... just really deep and it just hurt... like an ache... and I kept saying, I can't walk so fast, we need to stop... but she said, no, we need to get you home.

J: Helen, point to the part of your body where it hurt.

H: (points to lower abdomen-pelvic area)

J: So after you got back home, then what did you do?

H: I just locked the door and went to bed... my husband was out on the road, he won't be home for two or three days. So I just went to bed and slept. It still hurt the next day, but it was better. But I didn't feel very good... I felt kind of... like I couldn't eat... didn't want to eat... was kind of nauseated...

J: And how soon after that did you find out you were pregnant?

H: I didn't have another period after that... so it was maybe... five or six weeks. I thought I was just late because I didn't... I didn't feel very good. But that wasn't it.

J: Is there anything else that you can remember to tell us about the time in which you carried Marisa? Anything about that time at all?

H: Nothing except that I never felt good the whole time... I was just really sick, sick to my stomach all the time... I was not really sick, I was... just felt... food just nauseated me... all the time... and I didn't get along very good with my husband... but that was not unusual... I should have felt better than I did.

J: Was your pregnancy and the birth different with Marisa than it was with your boys?

H: Yes, in some ways.

75

J: How is that?

H: Well, I had no idea what it would be like. No one told me... and it was... it was a long labor, really difficult... for such a small baby... but then the boys, the next child, that was difficult but he was so big... so I don't really think it was unusual.

J: And when your boys were born, did you bond with them any faster than you bonded with Marisa?

H: Yes... that shouldn't have been... I should have bonded with her right away.

J: Just let yourself begin to go deeper and deeper, more and more relaxed, realizing that you've looked at many things this last session, discovered, re-experienced.... Just let all of that material become clearer and clearer, more and more in the next few hours, days, and weeks, and come forward for you to write down, remember. Your body is going to feel wonderful, relaxed, as though you've healed and accomplished a great deal. And the next time that I ask you to look high up into the back of your head and close your eyes, take a deep breath, you will immediately go five times deeper than you are now, easily and quickly into hypnosis, more and more comfortable. And you can begin to let your mind, your body, your spirit, your emotions all come back to a very comfortable, relaxed, balanced place. And as I count from one to five, bring yourself back very slowly....

Chapter 4

03/29/98:
Fourth Regression
with Dr. June Steiner and Helen

June (J):[1]Is the colonel's first name George?

Helen (H): I don't know. (fingers)

J: Is the colonel's first name Rich or Richard?

H: I don't know or it's not all right to say. (fingers)

J: Is there a good reason at this time why Helen is not able to recall the colonel's first name?

H: I don't know or it's not all right to know. (fingers)

J: Is the answer I don't know?

H: (not sure of response)

J: Just let the deeper mind do all the work. Let the deeper mind answer each question. I want the deeper mind to go back to when the colonel took Helen to visit the base. I want the deeper mind to look fully at the whole trip, at who went, at how they got there, the vehicle they took, and who else might have joined them. And just let the deeper mind remember clearly everything about that trip. And when I ask Helen in a few minutes to tell me what she knows about that trip, everything will come forward easily and clearly. When was the last time Helen had contact with the blue light? Was it within the last six months?

H: Yes. (fingers)

_____

1. *A subsequent regression--beginning of tape is missing.*

J: Good. Was it within the last three months?

H: Yes. (fingers)

J: Was it within the last one month?

H: Yes. (fingers)

J: Was it within the last two weeks?

H: No. (fingers)

J: Was it within the last three weeks?

H: No. (fingers)

J: Was it a month ago?

H: Yes. (fingers)

J: Did it occur when Helen was at home?

H: Yes. (fingers)

J: And when the blue light was seen, did anything else occur as well?

H: I don't know or I can't say. (fingers)

J: Helen has mentioned several times green bugs. Is there any connection between green bugs and Helen's experiences with the ETs or the hybrids?

H: I don't know or I can't say at this time. (fingers)

J: Is it that Helen does not know?

H: (unsure of response)

J: Thank you for answering my questions, and now I would like to ask Helen to tell me what she knows about how she got to the base with the colonel. Helen, I want you to go to the time when you traveled to the base where the colonel worked at Four Corners, where he met the hybrids, where he picked up the pieces of the ship, and where he met Raechel. Go to just before that trip took place and tell me what you're aware of.

H: (long pause)... I can't remember... I can't remember... making the trip... just... until just before... until just before going in the road... off the main road on the old road... on the old dirt road.

J: Was there a marking of any kind as you went off the main road?

H: Yes, there was an old cattle chute, a cattle loading... place, an old corral.

J: Was there anything written?

H: I don't think so.

J: Take a good look as you turn off at everything around you. Tell me everything that you see.

H: There's just an old corral, but it looks really small... and a lot of the fence... a lot of the posts are falling down, but you can see... you can see that they probably have used it not too long ago, but yet there's no tracks around the corral... but just past it is this old road that turns off to the right because that's where the corral and the cattle place... it's on the right-hand side of the road... just this old road that looks... is supposed to look it hasn't been used for a long time, but it has.

J: What is the road that you're turning off of? What's the highway?

H: It's the only highway south from... it's the only main highway south... from Ely.

J: And about how far from Ely have you come?

H: Um... maybe ninety miles, eighty or ninety miles. I didn't look.

J: Have there been any other important road signs along the way?

H: I don't think so... there was one before we turn off... there was one that says how far to Las Vegas, but I don't remember how far that was.

J: Then just take the small road. Let yourself, you're being taken down that small road, and tell me who you're with.

H: (long pause)... I don't know who I'm with... I haven't seen this person before.

J: What do they look like?

H: It looks like the colonel... but he doesn't have a uniform... and he has his fatigues on... not the shirt, just a T-shirt... just the T-shirt and the pants because it's so hot... it doesn't look like the colonel...

J: What do you mean, he looks like the colonel, but he doesn't look like the colonel?

H: Well, he says he is... but he doesn't look like the man I saw in the apartment with Raechel... but he's the same size... his face doesn't look the same.

J: Does his voice sound the same?

H: Yes.

J: How do you feel with him?

H: Well, he's been all right... we talked about the scenery and the ... he talked about it. I didn't say anything because I had a hard time keeping awake.

J: Why is that?

H: I'm so sleepy... but I'm... I'm awake now and I can see... it's like it is the colonel, but his face is different. The rest of him looks the same... and he sounds the same... I don't know how his face could change.

J: And did you sleep during part of the trip?

H: I guess so.

J: Were you tired when you started?

H: Not really... but as soon as I got in the car... I guess I must have fallen asleep.

J: Did you have anything to eat or drink in the car?

H: I wasn't hungry... He had some sodas... and I remember we got out of town... and he asked me if I was thirsty, and so I said, yes... and... and so he had a little cooler with some sodas in it, so he pulled off the road, got two cans out of the cooler, and he had one and I had one... and I guess I fell asleep after that... but that's a long time to fall asleep.

J: What do you mean?

H: Well, from Sacramento... clear to south of Ely... that's a long way.

J: About how long is that?

H: Five or six hours at least... I think... it's not much less than that.

J: And when you woke up did he say anything to you about having been asleep?

H: No, he didn't say that. He said, how do you feel? And I said, well, I guess I feel okay. I guess I must have fallen asleep. And he said, yeah, you were really tired. So I thought maybe I was. I must have been if I slept all that time. So then... we had turned off and we were... looked like we were going to nowhere in the middle of the desert on this old road... and so I said, where are we? And he said, we're almost there. It's just not very far, now. Well, I don't see anything (Helen said). Well, just wait... it's over... he says, it's just down... down behind this... this little... it was like a little hill, not very high, but then the road went down on the other side of it... and then, I could see... could see we were... we were there because it had a big, high fence around it. Really high.

J: About how high?

H: Maybe twelve feet, ten or twelve feet.

J: What was it made out of?

H: Heavy wire... like squares, heavy, real heavy-duty... and then it had like rolls, rolls of wire on top of that, up another, another foot or ten inches, or a foot, and that, I think, was electric. I don't know but I think it was. And there was a big gate, big iron gate.

J: Was it open or closed?

H: It was closed.

J: What else did you notice?

H: There was a guard there... and a big dog... and there wasn't any guard shack. That was... bases always have a guard shack... this one didn't. It had the gate and the man and the dog. So there was no chance the guard would miss anybody that came over that hill.

J: So then what happened?

H: We drove up. The guard walked out, the dog right beside him... and I rolled the window up because I'm afraid of that dog... and... the man who was driving took something out of his pocket and showed the guard. He just saluted and he didn't touch anything, but the gate opened. I didn't see him touch anything, but it must have been on his belt or in his pocket. The gate opened and we just drove through. I put the window down because it was really... it was hot.

J: How many were in the car?

H: Just me and him.

J: And then what happened?

H: We went on a little ways further... and it was just nothing but old... old barns and sheds... and another old corral out there behind... and so he just... just pulled in and there was a truck... two trucks behind... behind the barn. You couldn't see it from where... from the road, but if you drove around behind you could see two. And... we pulled in and parked, and he said, well, come on, get out. So I did. I could hardly move, I was so... I was really stiff.

J: And as you got out and closed the door of the vehicle, what kind of a vehicle were you riding in?

H: It was an old station wagon... I don't know what kind... a big one.

J: What color was it?

H: It was kind of brown... kind of brown and tan.

J: And what was the license plate?

H: I didn't see the license plate... because I didn't go behind it. I got out and I walked in front... and I didn't look back at it.

J: And when you were there, did you meet the two women who helped take care of Raechel?

H: I only met one.

J: What was her name?

H: I wasn't introduced. I mean... I saw her but I wasn't introduced.

J: So you didn't actually meet her.

H: Not really, no. I didn't. I was not introduced to her but I did see her.

J: How did you know it was one of the people who taught Raechel or took care of Raechel?

H: The man I was with said so.

J: And did you meet the other hybrid?

H: Yes.

J: And were you introduced to him?

H: Not by his name. Just... that he was responsible for... for helping raise Raechel... partly responsible. No name. It was as if nobody wanted me to know who they were. Just faces.

J: And as you looked at him, tell me what he looked like.

H: He was little, really slight built, not very tall... he looked sort of like Raechel. His skin was... his skin was sort of like hers... really smooth, really smooth-looking... and kind of... kind of greenish... greenish-yellow, but a little bit lighter than hers. And he had big eyes like her, but his were blue, really pretty blue.

J: Did you ever look into his eyes?

H: Yes, I did.

J: And what happened or what did you see when you looked into his eyes?

H: It was... his eyes looked friendly... and I felt that... I felt that he was thanking me... for being a friend. But he could talk, but he sounded squeaky, really squeaky little voice... and he didn't say so... not with his words, but he told me with his eyes... he didn't like to talk because the words weren't right, the words didn't sound right.

J: So you, too, knew how to talk without words.

H: Yes.

J: And where did you learn how to do that?

H: I could do it for a long time.

J: When was the first time you knew you could do that?

H: (long pause)... when I first... when I was a little girl... and they wanted me... they asked me if I would like to have a baby... and at first I talked... I spoke... but then I found out I didn't have to... just think and it was easier.

J: Did you continue communicating that way with them then over the years?

H: Sometimes... sometimes it was just easier that way... it was quicker. You just think, and they pick it up. It's easy.

J: Was there anyone besides the colonel and the ones that contacted you over the years that you could talk to that way or understand that way?

H: Oh... I think I could communicate with the ones that come now. I've been afraid to, but I think I can do it now. I didn't try before. I think I can do it with the birds now... I could do it with Raechel.

J: Did you ever do it with the doctor?

H: No, but she... she did it with me. She did both ways. She talked, she spoke, but at the same time she did it with her eyes.

J: And did you understand her?

H: I don't think I understood... saying... it was too loud... but I could turn my mind off... I didn't have to take what she said with her eyes.

J: Did you ever communicate with Marisa that way?

H: Not directly.

J: What do you mean?

H: We could do it long-distance. Wherever she was, she could think of something and I would pick it up, and I could do that to her, too, almost always... we didn't try... we just did it... she was really surprised at first, but she got used to it... and then after a while we hardly had to even call. We did... but we already had said what we said on the phone, then later... we said it first... with our minds... she wasn't sure sometimes, so she'd call me on the phone... and I'd say, I know that, you just told me that... then after a while, she just... she just got used to it.

J: Did Marisa ever question the fact that she could do that, what that might mean?

H: Oh, yes... it really scared her at first... and I told her there was nothing she could do about it... that it was just something that she... it was an ability that she had... and... she couldn't do anything about it... she couldn't stop it. And... that she had to get used to it because it would always be there... and she said, well, how do you handle it?... and I said, sometimes it makes me nervous, too, but... and I get really upset and I get frightened, but I can't stop it. And I said, it's really nice to be able to do this... it's a gift... think of it as a gift... but then she saw some really bad things happen... she could see... that was different, though. She could see things in the future that would happen... and that wasn't a gift.

J: What do you mean, it wasn't a gift?

H: Well, maybe it was… maybe it was a gift, but it frightened her really bad because most of what she saw were car accidents, people being killed, being murdered, things like that. She couldn't do anything to stop the things from happening, and… and that made her very upset… and it bothered me, too, but I didn't know what I could do about it.

J: Were any of your other children able to do that?

H: One is just starting now.

J: Who is that?

H: It's Carl… and it's very upsetting to him. He has too many other problems to deal with this now… but… he can't stop it… I mean, he can't do anything about it. He has to accept it. He sees things that happen in the future… I don't like to see that happening to him, but… but I don't know what I can do about it. I can't stop it for him. And I tell him he has to… he has to learn to live with it… because it's the way we are.

J: Helen, just let all that be. And I want you to go back again to the base with the man who helped Raechel speak. And tell me if there's anything else that happened with that man or on the base that you haven't yet told us.

H: I don't think there's anything else.

J: And I want you to get back into the car, the station wagon-type car that you came in. Notice if you see the license plate as you get in, or as you approach the car.

H: Oh, I still don't look at that… but I saw the one next to it on the… I look at the truck that's parked beside it, and it's a different truck than… than when we came… and it's parked out closer to the building. And I see the front license plate… and it's on… it's on the right… as I look at the truck, it's on… the left-hand side and that's not right. It should be in the middle, but it isn't. It's on the left-hand side… and it's the black license plate that I saw before.

J: What's on the black license plate besides black?

H: The triangle... and it's got the lines through it... it's the same one.

J: And when you see it, what do you feel?

H: I think, oh God, what is happening to me?... but it all begins... it starts to all get connected now somewhat.

J: Do you say anything to the colonel?

H: No. I don't let him know that I know. I just look away. I don't have to keep looking at it. I've seen it before. I don't want anything to happen to me. I want to get home.

J: Then after you get into the car, do you drive straight home?

H: I think so. I don't remember anything after going through that gate again. Not a thing.

J: What's the next thing you remember?

H: Getting into my car... at the parking lot at the apartment house where Marisa lived. By myself. I don't know... I don't even have... I don't even have any... clothes... any suitcase with me... I don't remember taking any... but if I did, I must have left it someplace because I don't have one now. But my clothes are clean.

J: Are they the same clothes you wore to the base?

H: No... someone must have taken my clothes with me, but... I didn't. I guess I changed them, I don't know. Maybe the girl did, but... they're not the same clothes... .well, anyway, I don't have the other ones with me... all I have is my purse... I don't know how long I've been gone. Well, I had to be gone... had to be gone two or three days. I don't know... I don't remember, but this man is not there... and there isn't any station wagon... and I didn't even go up to the apartment. I just get in my car and I drive home.

J: And when you get home, is there a calendar anywhere that you can look at?

H: There's one in the kitchen... but I don't know... I don't know what day I left... I must have missed work... whenever I went. If it was... three days, it would have to be three days... it takes a long time to drive over... and time to drive back and whatever time we were there... so no matter when I went, I had to miss work. But I didn't call in.

J: Did you ever talk to anyone about this trip?

H: No... no. Because I wasn't supposed to.

J: Who told you that?

H: The man I was with.

J: Did he say anything else besides for you not to tell?

H: No... he said I should never tell... I don't know... (long pause)... it just seemed like it was the colonel, but... but his face wasn't really quite right... when he said, you can't tell anyone, you can never tell anyone... his voice didn't sound at all like the colonel. I knew he meant what he said. I knew what he meant, too.

J: Did he ever say what he meant?

H: He said there will... no one will ever find a trace of you or your family if you ever say a word... and I said, okay, I will never tell... but I don't care now....

J: Why do you feel differently now?

H: What they're doing is wrong... what they did to me was wrong... they never asked me, they just did it... they messed up my life... messed up my daughter's... and I can't forgive them for that.

J: Just leave the trip behind for now, Helen. More will come forward if there is any more in days to come, weeks, months. And I'd like you to tell me if you have any reason to feel uncomfortable around bugs, especially green ones.

H: No... because they've never harmed me.

J: What do you mean, they've never harmed you?

H: (long pause)... well, sometimes they look scary, but... they've never done anything....

J: What kind of bugs are you talking about?

H: Ones with scales on.

J: And where have you seen them?

H: Well, I don't think they were real bugs... they're supposed to be like people... but they weren't... but they weren't green, either.

J: Have you ever seen green bugs that frightened you?

H: No.

J: Have you ever seen anything that looked like a green bug that frightened you?

H: Not green.

J: What kind of bugs have you seen that have frightened you?

H: Kind of big, long, brownish bugs with scales, but it was supposed to be faces... but I don't think there was a face... not a real face... like... like... like scales or... or the markings like turtles have on their shells. They overlap and they're kind of... kind of rounded things like they're all sewed on top of each other... they look... they don't look like bugs... but I don't know what else they look like... they're supposed to be people, but they're not people...

(blank spot in tape)

H: ...anyway... they didn't look... nobody noticed that they looked so strange....

J: Just let those two strange, different-looking people go out of your awareness, and tell me if you have ever been in contact with any other forms of life other than humanoids or the hybrids like Raechel and the man who helped her talk.

H: No... that was enough... that was enough.

J: And just let yourself relax and go deeper and deeper into a very, very wonderful place. A place where you can relax and let go, and let every breath you take bring more and more relaxation and healing into your body, your mind, your spirit, and your heart. And just feel with each breath more and more healed, and more and more relaxed. And know that everything that you have uncovered and recovered in these last few days will become clearer and clearer and you'll understand it better. You'll integrate it and be able to take it in, and it will help to improve your life. You'll be able to look at it without fear. Just let yourself float deeper and deeper and more and more relaxed. Let your body come back into a wonderful sense of well-being. Let your heart be light, your emotions be happy, your spirit be strong. As I count from one to five, you'll be coming back into the room this Sunday afternoon, on March 29, 1998, bringing back with you everything that you've learned, bringing back a new sense of strength to face whatever it is that you're learning. You'll remember everything that you need to remember to complete the journey. You'll come back knowing that you can go just as deeply back into hypnosis whenever I ask you to raise your eyes and then close them and take a deep breath and relax. So now, one, taking another deep breath; two, beginning to move the energy about your body; three, moving your hands and your feet, becoming more and more awake; four, feeling very, very much energized; and five, opening your eyes, feeling awake, refreshed, and very, very good.

"Doing extensive research, and finding nothing, is an answer too," —former intelligence officer.

Section 2

Chapter 5

Raechel Is Described
By The People Who Met Her

---

*T*he fact that Raechel was real and was at one time Marisa's roommate was verbally confirmed early in the investigation. There is a tendency for remembrances of others to mellow as the years go by but memories of Raechel seem to remain quite strong to this day.

12/10/98 Synopsis of a telephone conversation with a former boyfriend of Marisa's.

A former boyfriend remembers Raechel as, "unusual, with an otherworldly quality," "someplace else" in her thinking, didn't quite fit in. He said that she "sort of made sense," but seemed to have no fund of knowledge, and was "on a different wave-length." There was something unique about her voice, it was sort of mechanical-sounding.

12-15-98 A telephone interview with a former boyfriend of Marisa's.

"I do remember one of her roommates was a little bit... like unusual, I believe I met her there once. I kind of remember Marisa thinking that, she might have been a little unusual, a little different.... that she was... you know, like tuned in to other.... She might have been tuned in to something that might have been, you know... extraterrestrial or supernatural, or something along those lines.

"Marisa was wondering... she thought it odd or strange because of the way this woman talked about her experiences... She was maybe just a little bit disengaged, I guess, was kind of my impression. Maybe a little flat or... hollow or disengaged.... The one kind of fleeting recollection that I have of the one time that I met her, was that she was generally unremarkable, at least to me."

04-20-98 A letter from a former roommate and friend of Marisa's.

"I am fairly sure Marisa met this girl through the placement office at Lost River and was probably set up with Raechel through the counseling department. I know that because of Marisa's sight disability she was in steady contact with her counselor.

"When I visited Marisa that day at her new apartment I remember sitting outside together and she started telling me of this girl Raechel who had been her roommate. I remember my response to what she told me as being a bit "freaked out" as we put it in those days and remember we were laughing and I was telling Marisa to stop from time to time in disbelief (not of Marisa's story, because I do believe what she told me was true, but because what she was telling me was too weird).

"I remember her saying that this girl couldn't go out in the sun. That Raechel was reclusive and Marisa didn't socialize with her much (let's face it, Raechel sounded a bit strange). Marisa was a very social person and I think she puzzled over this girl's reclusive manner. She said that Raechel wore sunglasses and that her skin had an odd texture. She said, I think, it had a greenish cast to it. I remember her mentioning the girl only drinking water that came in containers. That Raechel didn't eat regular food and only special food that came in boxes. (Marisa and I were great food fans so this was important to us both, although Marisa had to watch her diet. We were both pretty health-oriented and lots of green vegetables and healthy stuff was important to us - so I know this was strange to us that someone couldn't eat fresh food we considered healthy). Like I said, I never went into the apartment Marisa and Raechel shared, so I never saw the containers.

"Marisa said that Raechel kept her body covered and protected from the sun. That was understandable in that we both knew people could have allergies. But the color and texture of Raechel's skin was what sounded creepy. And I think because Raechel didn't really ever talk that much about what she could or couldn't do made it feel creepy. If someone has differences it's a lot easier to accept if you know the reason, but when Marisa was telling me this, my feeling is that she was puzzled and not at ease about the whole matter. That's what brought on our conversation, not meanness or girlish cattishness, but discomfort with things strange and made creepy feeling because it was not explained.

"Marisa never mentioned anything about the girl's family to me. But I vaguely remember her saying something about odd visitors at the apartment. Odd in that the people who came to see Raechel were not other students like whom Marisa and I had friendships with.

"Then Marisa told me that the girl disappeared. That she didn't know where she went. That this roommate just was gone and Marisa had no idea where or why. Marisa was still shaken up over the episode, and I'm sure her husband (whom she married later on) heard a lot more of the story. I do remember him interjecting on the story to tell me it was true or something...."

10-26-97 Interview with Helen.

"Marisa was about 5'4" or 5'5", maybe, and it seems as though Raechel was just a little taller, not more than an inch. No more than 5'6". She probably weighed about 115 to 120. She wasn't heavy, she wasn't thin but... She had long legs, and long arms. The torso was relatively short. She was actually of an average build, it was just... just the facial features that were so striking. Her high cheekbones, too, and the color... skin coloring... was certainly unique. It was yellowish-green."

"Could that be like jaundice?"

"I thought of that, too, and medically speaking, it could be and it could also be from eating the green stuff, but in her case it was not an unhealthy color. It was a beautiful skin color, but it was so unusual. And the eyes, avocado-green, and their placement on her face. She was really a beautiful thing. I don't know, other people might not have thought she was beautiful, but I thought she was."

05-25-98 Interview with Marisa's husband.

"Once in a while I'd see her... Marisa and the strange one stayed together. I met her and saw her, she had hair, and then one time she says, yes, well, she's got no hair now. All of her hair fell out. I'd seen her with a full head of hair. Just seemed like it was short and not real long. The style back then was, it wasn't... it looked... I didn't pay that much attention to it... but Marisa says, yes, she's bald, completely bald.

"There was another incident where Marisa said it looked like Raechel had slit her wrists. Marisa said she had big scars across her wrists.

"Raechel wasn't attractive to me, so I didn't really pay any attention to her. I don't remember her being busty, or anything attractive.

"She didn't wear glasses. The first thing I usually look at on a woman, I like to look at their eyes and then work my way down. As far as her eyes, I don't even remember what they looked like. It's kind of like there wasn't anything to look at, so why even look the rest of the way down.

"I would say the image of her face would be just a face, nothing, nothing there, nothing. She looked to be Caucasian. The color of her skin was kind of on the light side. She was 5'5", 5'6"... somewhere in that range.

"Marisa said she had some really weird feelings about her, and when the men in black were there... she just said from then on, I'm not going to stay here with this, with her in the house, this is not safe, not so much Raechel, but as what was going on around her. Raechel was strange... but there were more things going on around Raechel, that dealt with Raechel, but that basically she had no control over."

06-06-97 Interview of Marisa's brother Carl remembering Raechel.

"I met Raechel, met her at my sister's apartment, upstairs apartment, many years ago. Quite an unusual gal. I remember dancing with her, hugging her, something... just cool skin, just kind of clammy feeling, just didn't feel right, didn't seem to feel right to me, and I don't remember what happened... I can't remember a whole lot of it. I think back, the more I think about it, the harder I think, the less I remember.

"I don't think she had sunglasses on. I know she didn't have sunglasses on. I don't remember her eyes other than they were set apart a little farther... and big old, big eyes. The more I think and try to go back in time and think about it, the more confused I get. I remember less of her than probably anything I've ever tried to remember.

"I want to say her eyes were black or dark brown, honestly, right now I'd like to remember, but it's just one of those things that I think I've got blocked, a mental block. I just can't draw anything out."

01-09-98 Carl remembers a little more.

"I remember going out with Raechel. We all went out one night, Marisa, her boyfriend, Raechel and I. I remember dancing with her. I don't remember where we went or how the evening progressed, but it was like a group going out, the four of us going out.

"She was awfully shy, awfully quiet. She was kind of a distant person, real distant, and when you dance with a woman you try to get a little close. She just didn't have the warmth.

"I wasn't really attracted to her, but yet, I don't know, she was just kind of cold to touch or feelings. She was more cold than warm.

"She was a very strange girl, very quiet, kind out of touch with everybody. I believe I only met her one time....

"She was smaller than me, thin-framed.... I want to say she had dark hair.... I want to say her skin was more like leather than skin, really cold... a weird-feeling kind of skin... when you're a young man in the service... but the skin was... was just kind of, it wasn't, didn't... she was cold to touch... she was almost like she was dead, kind of.

"I think it was more of being forced into dancing with her and being with her by my sister than anything. It was more of a setup so she'd have some company. I think that it was one of them "sister love" deals... all I remember is she was like a zero compared to girls I've been around as far as conversation and, you know, happy and bouncy, she wasn't any of those."

07-09-98 Helen is interviewed about Raechel.

"When Marisa first started talking about the food and stuff that she could drink, I suggested maybe she had some sort of a physical problem. That maybe she had to be on a particular diet because there are a lot of disabilities where you can only eat and drink certain things. Marisa thought it was sort of strange, and I did too, that when she wanted to try some of Raechel's food, Raechel said no, she couldn't, that it would make her really sick.

"Marisa started talking about the men that came to visit Raechel. She was in one of those periods when she could see a little bit better, and she looked on the boxes and discovered the logo. Then she found it on the jugs, and saw it on the license plate.

"After the colonel talked to Marisa of Raechel's origin, Raechel cut both of her wrists in an apparent suicide attempt. She received no medical attention for this, did not seek any--apparently she stopped the bleeding by the same technique she used when the colonel discovered her in the crashed vehicle."

The suicide attempt was also remembered by the man who was later to become Marisa's husband.

11-07-97 During a regression Helen remembers Raechel's eyes.

H: Well, her eyes were large but not like the usual picture, you know, like the picture on the cover of that book. They were not so high, but they came out onto the sides, because the glasses she had were the wraparound, you know, the old-fashioned ones. What really struck me was their color, avocado-green... that's the closest thing I can think of.

10-03-98 Regression with Helen and June, exploring Raechel's looks and actions.

H: She didn't fall like a regular person... she didn't bend, I mean she bent at kind of a funny angle. Another person would have tried to catch themselves, but she didn't know what was going to happen. She didn't know. Everybody falls sometime in their life. It's like she never did before... and so I knew I had to reach out and get hold of her. But this is so weird, that she just... well, anyway, I took hold of her. I got hold of her arm, but she didn't try to catch herself like a person would.

She just kind of fell over, like she would bend at the waist or something, it was really strange. Marisa couldn't see what was happening, she could hear it, but she didn't see. During this, while I was trying to get hold of Raechel and keep both of us from going on the floor, a lot of things started to happen all at once. From what I could see... because her glasses went down, I could see the eyes, and I could feel her arm. Oh, God... this is not like anything I've ever been in before.... Oh, but I can't drop her... I want to... I'm kind of afraid... I don't know what I've got hold of here, but... but I don't... I hang on... I looked in those eyes.... Oh, God....

J: What do you see as you looked into her eyes? Let yourself look deeply into her eyes. What is it you see?

H: Just that green... the whole thing... oh, it's like I go inside the eyes, but I'm not because I'm there.

J: Perhaps it's like when someone says the eyes are the window to the soul... and it's as though they're looking into the person. Is that what it's like?

H: Kind of... but there was no limit to what I could see.

07-16-99 In a subsequent regression, Helen remembers a few more details.

J: I want you to be there at that moment, Helen. You're reaching out, you're touching Raechel. I want you to feel it, and see it.

H: I don't like to...

J: Why is that?

H: Oh... because she didn't feel real... oh... she... oh...

J: Feel her arm and tell me...

H: Oh (crying out)... Oh, it felt spongy and it was cool, and it was a hot day. She shouldn't have felt cool, not that kind of cool, and it was spongy, and it... and I couldn't let go... because if I did, then she'd fall. Marisa couldn't see, she couldn't catch her, so I had to hang on... and she didn't go down. But her scarf slid, kind of back a little. Her glasses came down.

J: And what do you see? Look at her face.

H: Oh....

J: What's the first thing you see?

H: The eyes... big... big eyes... black slits....

Chapter 6

Trigger Events—Eyes and Windows

During Helen's regression sessions she would be answering questions, then suddenly skip over an event or say something that didn't make logical sense within the context of what was being said. When questioned about this leap in logic, she avoided the question, or had an unusual emotional reaction to what was being discussed. When pressed for details, she said she didn't know, or was afraid to say.

This may signal what is called a trigger event. Something else has happened at this point and the person under hypnosis doesn't want to deal with it. Saying anything that comes into their minds, they are often concerned about sounding foolish. They censor themselves, remaining silent about meaningful events. Taking the person back to the events just prior to the trigger event is a helpful technique. Key questions usually help to uncover skipped material or deeply buried material that the person has trouble remembering. Asking questions about material already verbalized can help get the person through the situation. When the person says "I don't know," restating the situation helps.

Using these techniques during subsequent regressions, a much more detailed experience concerning Helen's interaction with Raechel was revealed.

In an earlier regression Helen refused when asked to go to the place with the windows that she went to with Raechel. Dr.

Steiner did not pursue that line of questioning and proceeded on to another subject. In following regressions she takes Helen back to the windows and the same situation to explore this trigger event. During these regressions, still another trigger event is hinted at, then immediately glossed over.

10-03-98   Helen is explaining further about what happened when she went to visit Marisa, and Raechel was the only one home. While standing in the kitchen Helen looks into Raechel's eyes, then finds herself in the window room.

J: How did you get on the other side?

H: I don't know, it was like one minute I was on the outside and the next, I was on the inside. I went through it, but there wasn't a door.

J: I want you to freeze-frame that moment when you went through the window. And I want you to go deeper and deeper to that place where your cells and your being are in touch with what happened that allowed you to go through that window. Tell me what you were going through and how you managed to do that. Because your mind and your body knows what that is, whether you understand that or not. Just tell me the process by which you got through that window.

H: Um... I put my finger on the window, and she put hers on the other side, just on the other side of the glass from mine. She kept looking at me, in my eyes... and I felt all warm and... not hot... but all warm and... I don't know... a feeling... I've never felt like that before... but while I was still all warm... I was on the other side. But I couldn't do it until she touched her finger to mine on the other side of the glass.... It didn't hurt.... It should have.... It should hurt when you go through glass.

J: Did you feel anything at all going through?

H: Like I was really tall and long and thin.

J: Here you are, now, on the other side of the window, and where are you?

H: I'm in a big room, a big, round building. It looked like there are a lot of... all these rows of circles of... big circles... of windows... it looked like they went all the way around and then the ones towards the inside the circles, they were smaller circles. I didn't see any people in there. I don't know what she was trying to show me. She said I want to show you where I live... and it seemed a funny place to live. It looked like lab counters, or kitchen counters or something on... not the first two windows, like from the third one on in toward the center... but I didn't see any... any people or any things.

J: Was there furniture of any kind?

H: I stood there inside, between the first and the second row of windows... then from the third window it looked like counters but they went around to...I don't know where they ended because it was... a curve and I couldn't see beyond where it went around to...the curve, but it looked like there was... and that was on the side toward me, where the counters were. Then, I don't know if there were counters to... inside the windows to the right... but across... it's so hard to explain... but I could see... it was something lower and it looked like... like something to sit on, like benches against the wall... well, that's... that doesn't make any sense, but there was nobody sitting there. They were lower... they looked like benches. The counters were high, were... not real high, though, but where you could do something on, you could write, you could do something. But the benches... were on the opposite wall from where the counters were, oh, this is confusing.

J: Don't try to make sense out of it.

H: There were benches facing where the counters would have been if there were any, but there was nobody there.

J: How long did you stay in this place?

H: I don't think I stayed very long because I didn't feel comfortable there. It really wasn't very interesting, it looked really cold and bare. It didn't feel cold, but there was just the benches and the counter and the windows. I said to her again, well, this is really a funny place to live. She said this wasn't all of it, but she said, maybe we need, maybe you need to go back. Maybe Marisa has come by now, and I said, well, now I have to go back. Do I have to go back through the window again because I still don't see a door... and she said this time we're both on the same side, I'll just touch your hand.... I'll hold your hand.... You put your finger on the window just like you did before... and I'll just put my finger on yours, and then we'll both be back in the kitchen. She said don't be afraid, we'll go together... and then we did... and then, the next thing I know, she was standing across from me where she was to begin with... and I'm still there with my hand on the kitchen table, feeling... feeling how cool it was.

07-16-99 During this regression Helen remembers more about Raechel's eyes, and another trigger event is explored.

J: What do you mean black slits?

H: Vertical slits like a cat's eye... her eyes... oh... they're all green... the whole thing... I mean... other than the slits.

J: Have you ever seen eyes like this before?

H: I don't think so. I was... I wasn't really so much afraid as... I just didn't believe what I was looking at. I was fascinated, I couldn't take my eyes off those eyes... for a few seconds.

J: And what happened during those few seconds as you were looking at Raechel's eyes, Helen?

H: I could feel how frightened she was. She was the one that was frightened, not me.

J: Why do you say that?

H: Because she knew I'd seen what she looked like and she didn't want that... not yet....

J: How do you know that? Did she tell you that?

H: She didn't say it.

J: What do you mean?

H: She didn't say it in words... it was just in the eyes. She looked right back at me and she was so frightened that I was going to say something about it. She was afraid I would say something to Marisa... or if... I'm not sure why she was so frightened, but she was. Then I stopped being afraid of her... felt sorry for her. It wasn't because she looked strange. I wasn't sorry about that.

J: I want you to go to that place inside of yourself where you know clearly why you felt sorry for her. Tell me what you're aware of.

H: She was afraid I wouldn't accept her...

J: Accept her for what?

H: ...as my daughter... and I thought that was ridiculous.

J: How did you know that, Helen? How were you communicating with Raechel at that time?

H: The eyes.

J: In what way were you communicating with the eyes?

H: She just stared, just looked really deep, but not as deep as I had to look in hers. She wouldn't let me go.

J: What do you mean, she wouldn't let you go?

H: Her eyes just held mine and then I thought well, how can this be? How can this be? This is not even a person because she didn't feel right and she didn't look right... her skin was not right, it was that funny color. What kind of a sick joke is this, she wants to be my daughter.

J: Did you say anything to Marisa about Raechel at that time?

H: I knew I had to talk to her about it, but at that time I didn't know how to explain it to anybody else. I couldn't really explain it to myself. I thought I would get it straight in my mind and then I would talk to her in a day or two.

J: I'm going to count backwards in time now, Helen, to the moment when Raechel's glasses slipped down and you're looking directly into her eyes. Be there looking into her eyes, experiencing it directly. I want you to tell me about the word "window" of Raechel's eyes. What does that mean? Looking into her eyes... as you said, being pulled into her eyes... communicating through her eyes. You called them windows last time we talked about this in October. What did you mean?

H: It was like looking in through a window, to see what was on the other side. Like I went inside her eyes, but I didn't... I mean... not that time.

J: What time did you go into her eyes?

H: The next time I went back to the apartment.

J: Tell me about that.

H: I went to see Marisa that time. I think to take her something, doesn't matter... but she wasn't there, but Raechel was... and she said she didn't know when Marisa would be back. "I... do... not... know," was what she said.

H: I said, well, I have a little time. I can wait a few minutes. And this was in the kitchen and we both stood there. I should have gone in the living room and sat down, but I didn't. I stood there in the kitchen with my back up to that old... oblong table... that porcelain top or whatever, enamel top... and I stood there with my hand kind of behind me on the table... and Raechel was kind of by the refrigerator, between the refrigerator and the stove. And she told me that she didn't know when Marisa would be back. So, that was all she said for a minute, and then that was when she said, "I... wish... you... could... be... my... mother." And I said, "I can't, I can't be your mother." She said that it would be nice to have a mother like Marisa's. And I said "Well, maybe so, but it doesn't make any difference, I can't be your mother."

J: How were you feeling when you said that, Helen?

H: Awfully upset, my insides were just churning, and they shouldn't have been because I should have been able to say, well, this is really flattering, but I can't be your mother. I could be a friend. This is what I should have said to her, and I should not have worried about it, but I did. I was really, really upset because I had a feeling that... how could I?... but I did... I thought for a minute maybe I was her mother. I didn't think I was, I didn't remember having a child like that and I didn't have a child like that. She just kept looking and I just kept looking back. I shouldn't have done that, either, but I couldn't help it. That's when I went in through the window... the first window.

J: Tell me what happened.

H: That's when she started to talk about... she was going to take me to see where she lived... and then I was...I could see a lot of windows inside of each other. It was like circles, a big, round room, and it was like a maze is what I think, but the hallways didn't go different directions. They all went around in a circle and the outside circle had a little opening into the next circle, and then that one had an opening into the next one towards the center. I could see that from where I was on the outside. And then Raechel was on the inside. She said, "Well, come... on... in. I... want... to... show... you... where... I... live." I said "Well, this looks like a funny place to me. I can't. There's no way to go through." She said, "Put... your... finger... on... the... window." I said, "What good is that going to do?' And she said, "Just… do… it." Then she put her hand in the same place on the inside, and here I am on the other side, the same side as her, on the inside. It felt good in there, really comfortable, and yet, I didn't know why I was… what I was doing.

J: What was it like in there?

H: It was all white, really light-colored. Everything seemed to be all white, but there were… oh, let's see… I don't know how to explain it. Each circle, on the outside part of it… it was really weird. It had like a counter like they do in banks to write on. Little counters that ran along the inside of the outer wall. There was a little, narrow walkway, a corridor, and on the other wall of that same outer circle was a little bench. The counters and the benches weren't continuous, they were about four feet long and then there was a little gap before the next one. They were in little pairs… like a chair and a table, but if you sat on the bench, you'd be down too low, you couldn't write on the counter. I don't know what they were for.

J: Did you ever sit on one of the benches, Helen?

H: I don't remember. I leaned on the counter, though.

J: What happened when you leaned on the counter?

H: I felt like I was part of it, but I was separate. As soon as I felt like that, I raised my arm and it came right off, so I stepped back in the middle… no, I didn't step in the middle, I stepped in the space between that and the next counter. I didn't touch anything… just put my arms down at my sides and I didn't touch anything.

J: How many windows did you go through, Helen?

H: Just one. But I could see through, there were a lot of them. I don't know how that could be because the room didn't look that big around. There were so many circles of passageways to the middle. I couldn't see the middle. It should have been just a huge, huge place, but it didn't seem that big. It seemed to be round, maybe it was oval.

J: Just let your deeper mind look very carefully at everything that's there. Don't try to figure it out, just let your deeper mind take you deeper and deeper into the experience. I want you to look all around you. I want you to look at the windows, I want you to look at the shape and the size of the room. I want you to see whatever is in the room, just see... I want you to become very aware of how you feel as you're looking at the room and at the windows. Tell me everything that you're aware of.

H: I don't know where she is. I can't see her. I can't see anybody. Just all those circles or rows. I felt like I was not really in control. I felt like... like I was going to faint. I was light-headed. I didn't know if she was going to come back. I was afraid that I couldn't get out of there. But I didn't say anything. I kept thinking, I wish she'd come back and take me back... she didn't come for a while. Then when she did, I felt all right again. I didn't have that... didn't have that queasy feeling in my stomach and I didn't feel dizzy any more. But I was still there, where I had been in the first place... not... not touching the counter. I was still there with my hand, my arms right at my sides... because I didn't know what would happen if I touched anything more.

J: Helen, I want you to stop for a minute and look around and see the counters and the windows, see the shape of the room, and I want you to go back, as far back as you can and tell me if you have ever been in this room or one like it before now.

H: No. I've never been in one like that. I don't ever want to go back there. I was so afraid that I couldn't get back to where I should be.

J: Have you ever looked into the windows of eyes similar to those that pulled you in?

H: Not really... the eyes were not the same, but the colonel... he didn't really pull me into his eyes. He told me a lot of things with his eyes, but the men that came in the van, the first time... the one man... I didn't feel the driver, he tried to pull me in, but the passenger... he was staring but I don't think that he was... I didn't feel he was trying to pull me in but the driver was.

Helen had an emotional response to the counters, saying her hand came off the counters, then in other sessions saying "I kept my hands from touching the counters, I didn't touch anything. I didn't know what would happen if I touched anything more...." Why did she indicate that she was afraid that her hand wouldn't come off the counters? Hands normally come off a counter when placed on one. Did something happen when she touched the counter that made her want to avoid touching them? Frightened and resistant, Helen wasn't ready to elaborate at this time. However in the following session she relates, with some reassurance from Dr. Steiner, a bizarre and frightening experience concerning the counters, and her time in the oval room.

07-17-99 Exploring the very frightening "counter" trigger event.

J: In our last session we talked at length about Raechel, about the windows that you saw as you looked into Raechel's eyes and how you were pulled in and allowed yourself to go to that place; how in that place you knew what was being said, and you could communicate with Raechel clearly; and in that place you described the windows in a new way, more clearly and more defined than you had before. And as you defined those windows you talked about a counter and a bench in each window. I want you to be inside that place, an oval-type room. I want you to look around you, to be fully present there. I want you to notice the counter. I want you to walk towards the counter now of one of the windows, and I want you to reach out and touch the counter, and just let yourself feel and respond fully to the experience. And tell me what you're aware of.

H: Hm... it wants me to touch it... but how can a counter....

J: Just touch the counter, Helen.

H: I do. I am touching it... oh... I... it looks hard.... It looks like a piece of board... like a... like it's made of wood or plastic, but... it feels soft... not real soft, but... oh... it feels kind of like Raechel's skin... but it's warm, not... real warm, but where her skin was cool...

J: And as you touch the warm counter, what else happens?

H: It doesn't want to let go of my hand.... There's nothing.... It's not sticky.... It doesn't want to let go... oh....

J: Just let your hand be there.

H: I don't want it to be there.

J: It's all right, Helen, just let your hand be there. You've gone through this experience in the past and been all right, so let your hand be on the counter and tell me what happens.

H: Oh... oh... I don't know....

J: It's all right. Just go with it.

H: It wants me to move my hand farther, and... I'm afraid... oh... I'm afraid of the counter. It won't let go....

J: It's all right, Helen. Let yourself be with the counter completely.

H: I pull and I pull... it's like it's... it's like it's glued on... and I pull and I get one finger loose and the rest are stuck tighter... but I keep that one up that I pulled off, and then I pull another one, and then my hand is stuck tighter, the palm of my hand. I'm so... I'm really afraid... and I can't, Raechel's not there... I don't call.

J: And what's happening with your hand? Is it stuck?

H: It just feels really, really warm and it tingles all over... oh... oh... I don't know... I'm afraid... I'm afraid to let the hand stay on there.

J: But the hand is on there, Helen.

H: I know.

J: What's happening? Just let go into what's happening, one moment at a time. Just let go.

H: Oh... oh...

J: You're going to be all right. Go into the experience.

H: Oh... oh... all of a sudden... it just stops pulling, but I'm still stuck, stuck really tight to it... and I don't dare put my other hand on because I'm afraid that will get stuck, too... then I'll never get away... I don't know what it wants.

J: Ask it what it wants.

H: It wants me to stay... not there on the table, the counter... but it wants me to stay... it says it wants me to stay in that room... but there isn't really a room. It's just a whole lot of corridors that go around and around.

J: I'm going to ask you to stop right here, Helen. I'm going to count from one to three, and if during that time that your hand was stuck to the counter you were shown where here was in any clear way, or you were taken anywhere, you'll be able to go there at the count of three. One, two, three.

H: Hm...

J: What are you aware of, Helen? Where are you?

H: I'm not there anymore.

J: Where are you?

H: I don't know.

J: Just look around you.

H: I'm in a different room. This is not white... where the counters and the benches were was white... this is like...

oh... it's a funny color... it's like blue-gray... really dismal-looking... kind of cloudy.

J: Is there anyone else there?

H: Oh, yes... well, that's where Raechel went.... She's there... oh... she's... she says, come over here.... What's on this wall?.... It's a... it's a big room... it's like tanks...

J: Tell me more about the tanks.

H: They look like fish tanks... that's not fish in there...

J: What's in there?

H: Little babies... and they're so little... but they can see... just... just floating around...

J: Who is showing you the room, Helen?

H: Raechel.

J: And what is she telling you about this room?

H: She says, "This... is... where... I... came... from." I said, "I don't want to look at it. I don't want to believe this... this is... this is sick and it's bizarre." She said, "I... do... not... care...

FIGURE 7. HELEN'S SKETCH OF THE DOUBLE HIGH ROW OF TANKS CONTAINING FETUSES.

if... you... do... not... want... to... look... at... it... you... have... to. It... is... time... you... knew. You... do... not... have... to... remember... it... but... you... have... to... see... it... now." The babies weren't... weren't pink or white, they all had that awful greenish color.

J: Did anything else happen in that room, Helen, while you were there?

H: No. I just felt really sick to my stomach. I ask her if she can take me out, take me back. I can't handle this... I said I need to think about this.

J: Why did they want you to stay here, Helen?

H: I don't know, but I don't want to be there.... It's just... oh... I don't want to look at these things. They don't even look real, but they are. They're alive.

J: Is anyone attending to them, Helen?

H: No, they want me to do that and I can't do it.

J: What do they want you to do?

H: I don't know, they don't tell me that. She doesn't tell me. I said "I can't stay here, I can't look at these things. I'm sorry that this is where you came from, but there's nothing I can do about it. I can't do this. I have to go back. Marisa needs me. I need to take care of her. I don't need to take care of these things." She didn't like it when I called them things. She said, "They... are... not... things.... They... are... from... people... like... you." I said, "I don't care, Raechel. I can't look at these things, I can't stay here...."

J: And then what happened, Helen?

H: She just kept her eyes locked on mine. I say, "Raechel, I want you to take me back right now. I'm not going to stay here, this is not right, to bring me in here and show me these... whatever they are."

J: What are they, Helen?

H: They're like little babies, but they just swim around, and even the stuff they're in, it's greenish-colored, too. But I could still see that the skin was greenish, and the hands had four fingers like she had... they're all the same length, the fingers. I look at that. I don't want to be here. She says, "Well... it... really... does... not... matter... what... you... want... But... I... will... take... you... back... Maybe... we... can... find... something... else... for... you... to... do." I say, "But Raechel, I'm not looking for a job." She says, "It... does... not... matter... what... you... want." I say, "I don't want to argue and I'm not going to, but I want to go back right now." I just kept staring at her, and we didn't go back to the counters and the benches... We... I'm back in the kitchen.

J: Stay in the experience, Helen, totally and completely in the experience, and tell me what you did. Tell me what is going on in the moment.

H: I'm in the kitchen where I was to begin with... my hand is still on the table behind me... and... she's still staring at me, but she's not... she was... between the stove and the refrigerator. Now she's closer to me and she's beside the jugs of water. She's not touching me, she's just staring at me. I'm sick... I feel sick... I never... I've never seen anything like this. The babies, there were a lot of them, some were bigger, some were small, some were really, really tiny... just swimming around.

J: Does anything else happen in the kitchen that day that's important for us to know?

H: I don't think so.... It isn't as if... I'd really gotten my way... though I did to a point. I got back out of that God-awful place, but she says maybe I'm not what they're looking for, and I say I'm really glad about that. I don't want... I don't want to do... I don't want to be there again, ever.

Chapter 7

The Humanization Project

When Helen refused to take care of the babies in the tanks, Raechel told her they would find something else for her to do. Further exploration of the Humanization Project revealed Helen's role in it.

07-17-99 Regression.

June (J): I want you to go back to that time when Raechel said they may have to find something else for you to do because you don't want to take care of whatever is in those green tanks. I'm going to count from one to three, and on the count of three I want to know, did they find something else for you to do? One, two, three.

Helen (H): I don't think so... except I can, I could communicate with the colonel through my eyes... I could do it with Marisa and I could do it with the boys. What difference does that make to them?... or to her?

J: I want you to take a moment, Helen, and let yourself be fully in touch with why you have those abilities. Let yourself see and feel and know what it is that you're doing with those abilities and why.

H: I don't know... just that I can do... I can do these things, but well, what's the point?

J: I want to take you to another place, Helen. I want you to imagine that you're stepping into an elevator or going down deep into the middle of the earth, and as we go down deep into the middle of the earth, you're entering a new stage of trance, and in that stage of trance you're going to one of the compartments within yourself that you know is totally and completely safe from harm. A place where you know the answer to this question because you have been in contact with this entire experience in this place where it's been safe, and perhaps not let the rest of you know what's going on to keep you safe. I want you to continue down and I'm going to count from one to ten and at ten you're going to be down at the center of the earth and the center of your own being, to a place within yourself that has been allowed to know the answers, and your deeper mind has said it was all right for us today to go to that place to allow new information to come forward. One, two, three.

H: They don't... they don't want me to give up, but it's not much of a job, not much of a part.

J: What is the part, Helen?

H: I would have done it, anyway. Just to tell, to tell about Raechel... and about Marisa. That was my part... is my part, I don't know why it's such a big deal. I mean, it's like I was given an important position.

J: Why do they want you to tell about Raechel and Marisa?

H: They say that people will believe me. I don't know why that would be any more than anyone else.

J: Do they want this information to begin to come out?

H: Yes, maybe they know me better than I think they do, because they know once I start, I won't stop.

J: Who is they, Helen?

H: No one that I've seen or talked to, either, but I guess it was the people that were raising these things in the tanks.

J: How do they communicate with you, Helen?

H: Just with thoughts.

J: Are they of this planet, Helen, or do they come from somewhere else?

H: They're both places.... It's working here.

J: What's working here?

H: To do the raising of these things, but nobody knows. Nobody is allowed to know, except a few people. It's so awful that nobody really wants to know.

J: What is it that's so awful about it, Helen? Is it the actual way in which the babies are raised or is the end result? What is it that you say is awful?

H: I think it's the way they're raised. The end result is no worse than the children we raise ourselves. Sometimes it's better.

J: And what happens to these children after they're born?

H: They are adopted out. Some people know what they're getting, some people don't and that's when the trouble starts. They try to take them home and raise them but they don't fit in. Sometimes they just disappear.

J: What do you mean, disappear?

H: They're taken back. They go out to play or they go somewhere, maybe with a family, and all of a sudden the child is gone.... It never comes back.

J: Helen, what is the purpose of this whole project? The project the colonel worked with, bringing hybrids through, the raising of babies, the adopting them out, what is the purpose?

H: I don't know the whole purpose. All I know is just a little bit.

J: What do you know?

H: It's just a giant experiment to see if they could fit in... like to replace.

J: To replace what, Helen?

H: Real people.

J: Why would they want to replace real people?

H: I don't know. I'm not told that... that's what I don't know. What is the point of the whole thing?

J: The colonel never told you what the point was, Helen?

H: Not really.

J: What did he say?

H: He just said that she was part of the project... to see how far they could get. To see to what extent the emotions could be developed, but he didn't say why they wanted to do that, but he was part of it.

J: Is it possible, Helen, that... the different ways in which you're contacted through the men in the van, through birds, through music, through smells—are they in any way connected?

H: Yes, I think they are.

J: In what way?

H: To let me know I'll never be out of touch with them, I'll never be free, and just when I think I may be, it happens again, and so now I don't try to fight it. I'm not sure what the point is. It's not threatening to me any more, at least I'm not afraid of it. Actually I'm not even surprised.

J: Go into that space, that private, safe space where nothing is masked or hidden. Helen, what is the name of the Project?

H: The Humanization Project.

J: And the code name?

H: I don't know the code name. I was never told. But there is one.

07-18-99 Regression.

J: Is there anything else that we need to know about the hybrid children? Is there anything that would be important for us to know about it scientifically or philosophically that you're aware of?

H: Um... they have no soul, so many don't. They're creating so many problems.

J: You say so many don't. Do some have souls?

H: Somewhat, there's too much alteration, but I don't know what that has to do with the soul, but it seems to. The children don't have any souls. They want to kill people, they're not supposed to do that.

J: Who wants to kill people, Helen?

H: The children do. They don't seem able to think good thoughts.

J: Was this true of Raechel and Marisa?

H: No.

J: Why were they different?

H: I don't know. I guess they were the right combination and a lot of them are. But there's so many that go bad. But they usually program to kill themselves. They kill other people, but then they destroy themselves. I don't think this experiment is a good thing.

J: Do you know why it's being done, Helen?

H: Not really. It's just an experiment. That's all I know about it. But there is usually a reason for every experiment. You have a goal, and I'm not told of the goal.

Chapter 8

The Colonel, Helen,
and the Underground Base

Helen was puzzled as to why she seemed to know so much about
the Humanization Project and the underground base called Four
Corners. When questioned she would answer, "I don't know, but
I'm sure it's true."

One of the researchers was familiar with a government program called STARGATE. In this program participants were
trained in remote viewing to be psychic spies, able to travel to
places psychically, using their minds to reveal intelligence information that would not have been available otherwise. The
results were often phenomenal.

Remote viewing research began at the Stanford Research
Institute in California in 1972 and was funded by the CIA. In the
December 7, 1995, issue of *Nature*, vol. 378, the project is
described, "A $20-million 20-year US government programme
to employ and evaluate paranormal spying techniques...various
US government agencies secretly used up to six psychics at a time
to help locate hostages, track down alleged terrorists and help
drug enforcement officials.... The reviewers agreed that the
results were statistically significant."

Helen agreed to try remote viewing even though she
insisted she'd never been to the underground base. She was soon
able to point to a specific location on the map, assuring us it was
just a guess. During the first regression, only her deeper mind
would answer questions concerning the underground base,

although she did say she had been there. In subsequent regressions she seemed to recall a certain highway sign, and described some structures. Armed with the remotely viewed location marked on a map, and the new information, a volunteer investigator drove to the area. The sign and the structures were right where Helen had indicated. The investigator videotaped the area, and some other sites that had similar descriptions. When shown the tapes, Helen was able to pick the correct site. Due to the low clearance of the investigator's vehicle, driving down the road was impossible.

In the following pages, information on the Colonel, Helen, and their trip to the underground base comes out.

11-07-97 Interview with Helen.

"Well, it was surprising that the colonel would go into that much depth because I don't think that Marisa would have required that much of an explanation. She and Raechel got along well, as weird a relationship as it was. I don't think it really meant all that much to her to find out all this information. But I guess he felt that she should know.

"I feel you deserve to know the truth about Raechel. She is so much different from you and yet you two have become such close friends… and you've been wondering about her, too, because she doesn't act like your friends, doesn't act like you. She is not from here. I rescued her in a crash near Four Corners and for some reason I took a special interest in her because she wasn't like all the other ones who had arrived. She was like one who helped me, he knew how to sustain her life. For some reason I wanted to keep her with me. I knew about the Humanization Project which had never had a young person, I don't remember the exact word, but a young person…. I thought that maybe she would be a good candidate for that project. That's when I contacted ATIC about what had happened. They gave their permission, but they said I had to adopt her and raise her as a human. I didn't know how I would do this because I'm not married, and I'd never been around kids much. But I had help from everyone else there." These aren't the right words, but this is what he said to her.

"Marisa did tell her that she was still the same person she was the day before... earlier that day. But I think just because my daughter could accept it, Raechel was smart enough to know, and certainly Harry was, that not everybody else was going to, and those two girls were not going to be together the rest of their lives, either. Sooner or later Raechel would have to be out in some other situation. She would not be accepted, and she knew that."

07-09-98 Interview with Helen.

June (J): Did the colonel show any emotion when he was talking?
Helen (H): No.
H: It was on that trip, that bothered me. It was supposed to be the colonel and it didn't look like him. It was almost as though that was the true colonel, on the trip, but the features didn't look like the same one that I had talked to in the apartment....
J: How did you get in the car with him?
H: I don't know.

10-03-98 Regression.

H: His emotions weren't the way they should have been.
J: What were they like?
H: Cold... he seemed to be... warm, like a normal person... but when he looked at me, just before I got all this information, his eyes were really, really cold and hard, really piercing.
J: As you're looking at his eyes and noticing how hard and cold and piercing they are, what color are they?
H: Blue, I thought they were dark before, but I know now that wasn't right. That's what I was supposed to see. He said he had

worked in the Project with others and he had learned to communicate with them. When he told me that, I did not realize that I was being told the information with the eyes. I thought it was with a computer or something. He didn't tell me it was with the eyes, but that was how he was doing it. How could I have not.... Why didn't I know? But I didn't, anyway. But I'm sure, now, that's how he learned, from the others in the program, the adults at the underground base.

J: And how did you know you were at the base?

H: Because the colonel said we were.

J: Was there anything at the base that would let you know it was different from any other place?

H: It was underground.

J: Was there a fence around the base?

H: Yes.

J: And how did you get through the fence?

H: They opened the gate.

J: Who opened the gate?

H: The guard did.

J: Why did he open the gate for you?

H: Because he knew the colonel.

J: And how did he address the colonel?

H: Sir.

J: And did the colonel have to give him any identification?

H: No. He didn't, but he should have. But he didn't.

J: Did he say anything?

H: No, neither one said anything. They just looked at each other. The guard said, go ahead, sir.

J: At any time during that visit on the base were you given information by the colonel through his eyes?

H: Yes.

J: When was that?

H: When I first got there.

J: Tell me what happened.

H: He explained that this was where it all happened, where it all started.

J: Where what all started?

H: Where he had gotten Raechel, where they had lived, and how they had lived. How she had been brought up. But then he took me to the places, too. But it was more through the eyes.

J: He took you through the base with his eyes rather than taking you through the base actually?

H: No, he took me actually. I didn't go to all those places actually, but I was there and he described it through his eyes, with his eyes.

J: And where were you when he did that?

H: I don't know. I was in the first place that we went into which was under the ground, but you had to go in through an old barn door. I don't know why he took me there because I didn't get to see much. He took me downstairs where there were a lot of rooms, where the people stayed, like a barracks, but they were all separate little rooms. And he took me in and he said this is where you'll stay. I was tired from the trip and I sat down on the bed... and that's where I got a lot of information about the lab. I didn't really go in there, in the lab. But I knew what it looked like because he made a picture in my mind, where I could see it.

J: Why did he want you to know about those places?

H: I don't know. If he took me there, why couldn't he have just shown me? Taken me in and let me look? I think he was not supposed to do that. I think it was all right, well, not really all right that I was there, but it was as far as I could go... as far as he could take me. There was nothing that would stop him from putting the picture in my mind because nobody would know.

J: Why would he want to do that?

H: I don't know.

J: Remember his eyes. Let yourself remember looking deeply and intently into his eyes. Remember you beginning to receive the information and remember anything at all that he said about giving you that information and why. What was the purpose?

H: Because I was Raechel's mother. But that's not what he said.

J: What did he say?

H: Originator.

J: What was the word?

H: Originator.

J: Originator.

H: And I never heard the word used like that before. And so I asked him back, what are you talking about? And he said, that's where she originated, with you. So you need to see what happened after I got her. I don't like being called an originator... but I guess that's what I was.

J: How old was she when the colonel got her?

H: Thirteen or fourteen. He was not exactly sure.

J: And why was he given the care of Raechel?

H: Because they'd taken something from him and added it to her. He didn't say what.

J: So the colonel was related in some way...

H: Yes.

J: Was the colonel Raechel's father?

H: In a sense... that was after they'd taken her from me. He didn't go into detail on it. I don't think I asked. I couldn't believe it. It was true, but he was not her only father.

J: What do you mean?

H: Because there were things they'd taken from the others that they added to her.

J: From what others?

H: Some of the others that were where she'd been after they took her from me and before she got there. I don't know where that happened. I don't where it happened when they took something from him.

J: Was that different than the way most hybrids were created, or is that typical?

H: I don't think that was typical. I think it was a new experiment.

J: What was the purpose of the experiment?

H: To see how well she could fit in. How an entity like that could fit in with normal humans, what their reactions would be, what they could feel, would they be accepted? But they messed up with her because she was pretty good on all the counts except the color of her skin and her eyes. Otherwise they did a pretty good job.

J: What was the purpose of creating a hybrid that could fit in with the human process?

H: He did not give me a reason for that except it was something the government wanted to do. He said it was a necessary thing and it would never stop.

J: What do you mean?

H: I don't know how many governments it was, but I think it had to be beyond our government. It had to be other civilizations, other planets, but I don't know what the purpose is... was.

J: I'm going to count from one to three, Helen, and I'm going to ask you during that time to go directly to the colonel's eyes and ask what was the purpose of this program... to have hybrids in with the humans. One, two, three.

H: He said they were not strong. They needed a breeding program. It's all it was, just a breeding program. Just like when you raise cattle, you take the best ones and mix them together until you get what you want. They wanted hybrids that were

126

physically strong, with good immune systems that they could get from humans. They wanted some emotions, but not destructive ones. They wanted to hang onto the intelligence they had. And they had a hard time getting everything mixed up just right. Raechel was the closest that they had come.

J: Why was the United States government involved in this?

H: He did not say. He knew... but he did not tell me that.

J: How long did you stay at this base?

H: Not very long, I think maybe twenty-four hours or less. But I seemed to have lost track of time.

07-17-99 Regression.

H: Helen, I want you to go even deeper and take yourself back to when you were taken onto the base by the colonel. I want you to be there in the moment. Tell me what's happening to you and tell me anything at all that would help us to understand what was going on at the underground base and the reason for it. One, two, three. Where are you, Helen?

H: I'm in where they eat, in the mess hall, but there wasn't any food right then.

J: Be there in the moment, Helen. Take yourself as deep as you need to go.

H: Some people come in, not very many.... There's a guard... his dog... I'm afraid of the dog... and it comes up and licks my hand so I guess it's all right, but I'm still afraid... and there's a woman... and she's a nurse.

J: What's her name?

H: I'm not told her name and anybody's name. It isn't very polite to introduce you to people and they don't tell you their name, but that's how they did it.

J: Were you told anyone's name while you were there, Helen?

H: No, it was like, this is the guard, you met him at the gate... and this is the nurse. She's the one who took care of Raechel and helped me with her.

J: I want you to be with the nurse right now, Helen. Let yourself go as deep as you need to go to be in the presence of the nurse. Look at her, tell me what you're aware of. Where are you?

H: I'm still in the same place and she's looking in my eyes. But she can't talk with her eyes. She just looks, her eyes are sad as if she'd like to tell me something, but she can't. She says I hope everything goes well for you. This is a funny thing to say when you meet somebody... I hope everything goes well for you....You should say, I hope you have a nice time here or glad to meet you, not that, it sounds strange.

J: Helen, why did the colonel bring you here today?

H: He wants me to know that although I'm already aware, well somewhat... of Raechel's origin, that it was just regular people that helped him with her. I wasn't worried about that. He didn't have to do that. He wants me to know that there really is a place like this. But then he tells me I can't go in the underground part because there are some things that even he can't do... is not allowed to do. And that's one of them... so, he just tells me about it with his eyes. He said, this is the best I can do... this is as close as I can take you.

10-03-98 Regression.

J: Did you ever see the colonel again?

H: I've seen the same eyes.

J: The same eyes as the colonel's eyes?

H: Yes.

J: Where did you see them?

H: The man in the van.

Chapter 9

Helen, Her Mother, and Her Aunt

If a person suspects an abduction, has repeated UFO sightings, and other unexplained experiences, there is a good chance his parents or children have had similar experiences. Members of Helen's family were interviewed to see if they had ever had any unusual experiences.

Many abductees tell of miscarriages and abnormal pregnancies. Did this apply to Helen as well?

06-21-98   A letter from Helen.

"On June 21, 1998, I talked to my aunt in Florida and asked her again what she had seen in the sky as a child (she's now in her 80s). She told me that her mother would get all the children up and dressed so they could go outside to see the 'lights and things.'

"Apparently the house and windows would usually rattle and shake when the lights appeared, though not always. My grandmother would tell the children that it was just like what she remembered happening to her home when she was a child in Switzerland. She told them it was probably an earthquake. They lived in upper New York State and I don't believe there were any earthquakes at that time, certainly nothing that could even have been detected, rattle the whole house. When they went outside, my aunt recalls seeing many lights and objects, various colors (red, blue, and green) and shaped in round, oval, triangular, and some that changed form as she watched. Some came in very low and she wouldn't go into any more detail on that. They flew alone and in formation, and all the children were really fascinated. My grandfather never saw them—he refused to get up and go outside or even to look out the window—told them all they were crazy."

10-03-98   Regression.

June (J): I'd like to ask you about your own mother. Tell me what you're aware of.

Helen (H): She really didn't want me.

J: How do you know that?

H: She told me that.

J: What did she say?

H: That she'd never really wanted me. I was never her child.

J: What did she mean, you were never her child?

H: Nobody will tell me. She wouldn't tell me.

J: Did other people ever say that you weren't her child?

H: No, it's so bizarre.

J: What's bizarre?

H: I think the woman who is my aunt is really my mother. My mother told me about ten years ago that I was never her child, that she didn't want me, never wanted me, never wanted any more contact with me. She wouldn't talk to me after that and then she got to where she had somebody from my brother's family there all the time and I never could get through to her. I was not allowed to talk to her, so I talked to my Aunt Helen. I told her about it and I told her it was so strange. She was always so much closer to me than my mother, the woman I thought was my mother. I asked, are you my mother? And she said, it was just so long ago, I don't want to talk about it. She won't talk about it, either. So I don't know, I wish she was my mother. She's a lot nicer person.

J: Helen, I want you to go into your deeper mind, and I want to ask your deeper mind to answer some questions about your birth... about your conception. Go as deep as you need to go to be in touch with that information. When you were conceived, Helen, who was the person in which you found yourself? Now I'm going to ask a question of your fingers. Was the woman who was supposedly your mother, your real mother?

H: (no - fingers)

J: No. Was your aunt your real mother?

H: (no - fingers)

J: No. Was your real mother someone who gave you up for adoption?

H: (I don't know - fingers)

J: I want your deeper mind to become very aware of the first time you were aware of the mother you thought was your real mother. Was it under the age of one?

H: (no - fingers)

J: No. Was it under the age of two?

H: (yes - fingers)

J: Yes. Was your conception a normal conception?

H: (no - fingers)

J: No. I want you to be very, very clear looking at your conception so that you know what wasn't normal about it. Is it all right for Helen at this time to talk about her conception?

H: (yes - fingers)

J: Yes. Helen, tell me what you're aware of about your own conception.

H: It was... oh.... It's so mixed up... so mixed up.... Oh... they took... oh, God... they take an egg from my aunt.... They do something with it.... Then it's put in my mother.... She carries me.

J: What was done to the egg and who did it?

H: I can't see, but I'm all mixed up.... My aunt can't have children.... She can't have children. She has no uterus, she can't have children. That's why, because they want to use her... they did what they could... they took the egg.

J: Who's they?

H: I don't know... but they took what they could from her, they didn't know that she couldn't have children, that she couldn't carry a baby until after they made the plans. I guess I belong to both of them, sort of. No wonder my mother said that.

J: I'm going to count from one to three and on the count of three, Helen, I want you to tell me who "they" were who took the egg from the aunt and put it in your mother. One, two, three.

H: I think they're the people who used to come with the blue and green lights that I saw when I was a child, but my aunt saw them when she was a child, too.

J: Tell me about the blue lights and the green lights.

H: They were like the lights that I saw when I went with Raechel. They looked like that. My aunt described them like that, too, but she saw crafts, and everybody did in the family, all her brothers and sisters. I think it was the people that came in those crafts that were responsible for what they did to her and me, and to my mother.

J: How did you feel when you saw the blue lights?

H: Fascinated, they were so pretty, the most beautiful shade of blue.

J: And did anything else happen during those times when you saw the blue lights?

H: I don't think so. I was a child when I saw them. The lights were a long way away.... I thought they were. When I talked about them, everybody said they were northern lights, but they were not northern lights, they were totally different. They were something that appeared on a pretty regular schedule.

J: Was there anything unusual about the way they would act?

H: No, they were not coming through the sky. They were already on the ground, but they must have been enormous. You could see so much light and they had to be quite far away, so beautiful. They were not northern lights.

Chapter 10

Helen's Pregnancies

In an earlier session Helen said she went for an evening stroll with a woman she didn't know. When asked why she would do this, all she could answer was, "I don't know, it doesn't make sense." Helen said she hated women doctors because they always hurt you. Dr. Steiner asked why. Further explanations on both these questions came up unexpectedly during the following regressions.

10-03-98 Regression beginning with Helen stepping back away from Raechel and touching the kitchen table in the girls' apartment.

J: Tell me about that kitchen table, Helen. I want you to feel the coolness of it and your hand on it. I want you to tell me if it reminds you of anything else. Have you ever felt that same texture, substance, coolness?

H: Same coolness, like in an operating room or exam room.

J: I want you to imagine yourself in a operating room or an exam room with that kind of coolness and tell me what comes to mind.

H: Awful lot of pain....

J: Where do you feel the pain?

H: (demonstrating)

J: In your pelvic area?

H: Um...

J: What's happening?

H: I don't know for sure, but they're doing something.

J: Who's they?

H: Supposed to be a doctor... supposed to just give me an exam but... this is more than an exam....

J: Tell me what you mean.

H: I feel like they're putting something inside of me.

J: What does it feel like?

H: It hurts, it hurts really bad. I think they're putting... I don't know.

J: What are they saying to you as they do that?

H: They tell me to hold still, be quiet, it'll be over pretty soon.

J: Do they tell you why they're doing it?

H: They say I'll feel better, and I tell them I felt good when I came in here, that I feel terrible now. They say, it doesn't matter, you'll be all right, you have to do this. Nobody will ever know after it's all done.

J: What is it they won't know?

H: What they're doing. I don't know what it's called, but they put something up inside my cervix. Because it hurts when it's opened up. But they tell me this is all right, this is okay, it's not going to do any harm. No one will ever know the difference.

J: No one except...?

H: Me.

J: You. What is it that you will know about the difference?

H: That Marisa is not entirely human.

J: And how does that feel to know that?

H: Not very good... not very good.

J: Do they tell you how you will be able to deal with that?

H: No, they said that at first she would be very, very much like any other child. They said since this is your first child, you won't know the difference anyway. And I guess they were right... in a sense.

J: What were those things you were aware of, however?

H: She was really small, but that's not unusual for a baby. She didn't eat very well and she didn't feel, her skin didn't feel just right to me.

J: How did it feel?

H: It felt always quite cool. But she was healthy, and it felt a little spongy, not much, but it didn't feel like it should. I didn't want to think that it was different, but I didn't want to remember what they'd told me, either.

J: So what did you do with that memory?

H: I put it away.

J: When you looked in Marisa's eyes, what did you see?

H: I didn't see anything there. Just love, just like an ordinary child.

07-18-99   Regression with Helen.

J: And move forward again to the very first time you, Helen, were given the opportunity to be the mother of such a child, let your deeper mind be fully aware of how it happened... and tell me what you're aware of....

H: I'm on the exam table. I don't want to be there. They say we'll just give you a checkup. That's when I tell them I don't need a checkup, I feel good. Then the blue light, that's when I see the blue light.

J: Who's there with you, Helen?

H: The lady that I went for a walk with.

J: Is that Rosalind?

H: No, Rosalind is the doctor.

J: Is she there, too?

H: Yes, but I only see her for a minute. She's not very nice. And I can't move because the blue light is just brighter and brighter.

It pushes me down because I want to fight. I want to get off the table. I'm not tied down. The light comes closer and closer and then I can't... and it hurts... they say it's going to be over in a minute and you'll be fine. Then the light... that's all I remember, but when I wake up the light is not there. But the lady that I came with is.

J: And who is that?

H: I don't know her. I see her in the neighborhood... and I've seen her before, too. I've seen her at some of the dances we played for and some of the shows. She would be there and she would come over afterwards to me and say, how are you? I enjoyed you tonight. I'd say, thank you, and that would be all, but she would come. I saw her two or three times. I'd go for a walk sometimes and I would be down the street and she would always... people don't do that... they usually don't speak, but she always said hello, how are you? So she knew me.

J: And did you have a child, Helen, nine months after this experience?

H: Yes.

J: And who was born?

H: Marisa.

J: Helen, I want you to move forward in time to the very next time that you were inseminated or impregnated. Let yourself go there and be fully in the experience, telling me what happened.

H: That's when I think I am having a miscarriage. I think I am. I went to work. I didn't feel good. My stomach hurts but I go in because I need the money. I know I'm just going to bleed all over, I can feel it coming. So I go into the nurses' lounge and there's a cot in there. Well, maybe if I lie down on it I'll feel better, but I don't. One of the nurses comes in. I don't remember her name, but she sees what's happening and says, "I'll get you some help." And I think she's gone to call a doctor... well, she does call a doctor, I guess. But I did not go to the hospital. I should stay right there, but the next thing I know, I'm in the doctor's office again.

J: Which doctor is that, Helen?

H: Oh, it's Rosalind. And she said, "I'll take care of you." I say, "I need a D&C but you can't do that here." "Oh, yes, I can do anything I need to do... no, whatever I need to do, I can do that...," and she's saying this in her German accent—vatever I need to do. And I said....

J: Stay fully and completely in the moment.

H: I say... "I don't care. I just want to feel better," but the blue light comes again and I know they should be doing something different than they are. Because I know how a D&C is... and it's sort of like that. She's taking something out, but she's really careful with it.

J: I want you to see what that she's taking out, Helen. Look at what Rosalind is doing and tell me what you see.

H: I'm not sure what the instrument is, but she's really, really careful, she uses two things. It's like something to go up inside and then something like a spoon. That's not it. It's something. She's really careful, she's not going to spill anything that comes out.

J: How does it feel as she does this? How are you feeling?

H: Well, by then, I don't feel very much because the blue light is there. Yet somehow I know she's doing more than she should be. And there's somebody else there that's not a doctor, but it's not a nurse, either. It's somebody, some lady with a gray suit and I become aware that this is really a strange thing. You shouldn't be wearing nice clothes in a place like that, because you would ruin them. But anyway, Rosalind takes both things out and she has something in the little spoonlike thing and the other lady has a little dish. She says, take this, you know vat to do with it. And I don't remember anything for a few minutes. When I wake up I'm on a little couch and Rosalind is not there. But the lady in the gray suit is. And now, it's the same lady that took me there before. She says I'll take you home now.

J: I want you to go into the blue light. I want you to ask for information now, Helen, about how hybrid children are created. What is it that you know about the creation of hybrid children? And when you're clearly aware of that information, tell me what you know, let the blue light speak through you with that knowledge.

H: It happens sometimes when you think you're having a miscarriage. They like to have a fetus already started, but then that makes it difficult because they have to change it.

J: How do they do that, Helen?

H: I don't know exactly. They take out, they remove some... I don't know what DNA... they take some DNA out sometimes, but not very often. Usually they insert some, what they do most often is take the egg from the woman and mix it in a dish with... just like we do with artificial insemination. Then sometimes they put it back in the same woman they got it from because then it'll grow okay. When they can't, when circumstances aren't right, they have to do it in the tanks after it's too big for the dish. I don't like to think about it.

Helen has had three or four apparent miscarriages. Each one occurred during the latter part of her first trimester. There were no obvious reasons for the losses.

Chapter 11

Raechel's Origin

Helen consciously remembers being given information that Raechel was not from Earth, and that she didn't seem to have a real mother and father. Exploring this further revealed an interesting and startling turn of events.

10-03-98 Regression. When Helen first meets Raechel.

H: That was when I thought I was having a miscarriage... and I went to this lady doctor.

J: Was this your regular doctor?

H: No, she wasn't. I knew her because she was a doctor where I worked at the hospital. I don't know why I went to her. I should have just had one of the docs there take care of me, but I didn't. Anyway I went to her office and it was a funny room, too. Not much furniture, but tables and things, not much in there, and it was really old. She said, we have to do a D&C, and I said, I want to go to the hospital. And she said, no, we're going to do it here. I said I don't want to do that. I work there, I can just go and you can... we'll just do it there. No, I have to do it here, and I have to do it now. She pushed me back down on the table. It was cold and hard. I guess it was her nurse that held me down and strapped me down. I thought they just did a regular D&C,

but I don't think so. I think they took out what turned out to be Raechel later on.

J: What symptoms were you having before you went to see the doctor?

H: A lot of cramps and my stomach hurt. I was kind of nauseated, too... but I guess I was probably at least two months.

J: Did you know you were pregnant?

H: I thought I was, but I wasn't sure, then I started to get cramps and a backache, and started to bleed a lot. I don't know why I went to her. She wasn't my doctor. I should have stayed right in the hospital because when it started I was already there and I worked for the operating room. But I had gone in the nurses' lounge and I laid down on the couch and somebody said... well, you just lay down... you just lay there and keep your feet up, and I'll go get the doctor. And I thought that they were going to get my doctor. And then I don't remember going to her office, but I was there, her office was maybe three or four blocks away.

J: Had you ever seen this doctor before?

H: Oh, yes, several times. She did a few little surgeries there. Nobody liked her very well. She was not very pleasant, but I think she was a good doctor. She just wasn't a very nice person. And she wasn't very nice to me. After we got through in her office I laid down for a little while on the couch until I felt better. Then I walked home... and I never went to see her again. I saw her again, but I never went to her.

J: Where did you see her?

H: In the hospital. Where I worked.

J: Did she acknowledge you when you saw her?

H: Not really. She would say, hello, how are you? Just like you would speak to a stranger.

J: Helen, I'm going to ask your deeper mind a question here. And I'd like your deeper mind to answer with your fingers before you speak about it. Deeper mind, I'd like you to go as far inside of this experience of having carried Marisa and carried Raechel, and I want you to tell me if you have knowledge of why you were allowed to give birth to Marisa, but that Raechel was taken from you and raised somewhere else. Do you know why it was done that way? Let your fingers know. Do you know anything about the difference in possible cell or tissue or DNA between Raechel and Marisa?

H: No.

J: Were you ever told by Raechel or the colonel or anyone else why Raechel was taken from you and then reintroduced to you when she lived with Marisa?

H: Yes.

J: Tell me about that.

H: That day in the kitchen when I talked to Raechel, when she talked to me. She said... I... have... never... had... a... mother... I... do... not... know... what... a mother... is... supposed... to... be... but... Marisa... talks... about... you... all... the... time. She said that she wished that I was her mother, and I said, I really can't be, what happened to your mother? And she said, I... never... had... one. Where... I... come... from... we... do... not. I... want... to... be... like... Marisa... and... have... a... mother. I... think... you... would... be... a... good...mother. And I said, "Raechel, I am not your mother," and then she said, "Well, maybe you do not remember.... No," she said, "someday you will remember." I said, "I don't want to talk about this any more." And that is when she said, "Well, let me show you where I live," and that's when I went to the window place. It's ridiculous. I didn't want to talk about it with her because I didn't think I was her mother but yet, I knew I was.

Later in the regression, Helen reveals more about Raechel's early years.

J: Did they tell you how they sustained Raechel's life at all?

H: She was raised in a vat, like an aquarium.

J: With liquid, you mean?

H: Yes, yes, with liquid. I don't know what kind.

J: How do you know that?

H: It's more information I got. I don't know who gave it to me. I think she did.

J: When would that have been?

H: That would have been that day I went behind the windows.

In another part of the same session, more information on Raechel's youth emerged.

H: ATIC wanted, insisted that he adopt her and raise her as a human. He had no idea of what to do with a child, never been around children. He didn't know if he could do it and he laughed, not laughed, because he wasn't a person that laughed, he kind of smiled. Then with sort of a smile, he just looked, just riveted his eyes on mine and all of a sudden, all this other information that would have taken at least a couple of hours to tell in words, all of a sudden it was there.

11-07-97 Interview with Helen telling of a telephone conversation with Marisa.

"She called me at work and was very upset at what had happened. I told her I would try to make some phone calls and see what I could find out about the father, if he had disappeared also. I did, and found out that he had disappeared without any apparent trace.

"She had called the college and there was no record of Raechel ever having been there. All her files had mysteriously disappeared, too. They said that all her records had disappeared. She didn't call administration. That they were aware that Raechel was a student there, and they were surprised that the records had disappeared."

Worried about Marisa's safety, Helen calls Jim, a friend who works in security at Highland Air Force Base, asking him to check on Colonel Nadien. At this point she takes a piece of paper and jots down Jim's name and phone extension number. She also takes notes as she talks with Jim. By sheer chance, at the end of their conversation, she tucks the note away, rather than tossing it in the trash. More than twenty years later Helen runs across this note hidden in some other papers. This note provided the researchers with valuable leads, including the base extension number that was still in use. The following is a transcript as she remembers it, when Jim calls back with the information he has found.

Jim (J): I hope you're sitting down for this. The colonel and the daughter came here from Four Corners. He was attached to one of the black projects much, much higher than Blue Book. He was there for a long time and was commander of the detachment. Your suspicions about the daughter are probably true, but I can't tell you that for sure—you know what I mean. The whole thing is pretty exotic, the outfit he was working for, ATIC, Aerospace Technical Information Center. And the men you mentioned, sounds like Men in Black, almost like something connected to the Nation of the Third Eye.... I don't know. But I couldn't say if I did, either.

H: Are you sure about ATIC? I've never heard of it, and as we're talking, I'm trying to find it in my listing of acronyms, but it's not here.

J: Yes, I'm sure that's it, and I'm sure, too, that you won't find it listed anywhere because it's not supposed to exist, but take my word for it, it does. And take my word for it, too, that that girl living with your daughter is most likely something the colonel got out of one of those craft that come to Four Corners. And something else, too. If you ever mention one word about this conversation to anyone, ever, I'll deny the whole thing. I have no choice.

H: I really appreciate your honesty, Jim, and I can't imagine who I would ever tell this to, or what I'm going to do about the situation, either. I guess nothing for the time being.

Upon searching the base archives it was verified that Jim did work in security at that time. An Internet search and examination of the property tax records, old telephone directories, and other databases in the California State Library revealed Jim's present-day address.

05-30-98 Summary of a telephone interview with Jim.

Jim said he retired in 1987 from Highland Air Force Base, after spending 24 years as a criminal investigator, "same desk for all those years," in the base security police. He said he did some routine background investigations, but was primarily occupied with theft of government property cases.

When asked if he remembered Helen having asked him to verify Colonel Nadien's position, etc., at Masters, he said he had no recollection. He said every secretary from time to time wanted him to check on something, and that it could very well have happened, but that he had "no memory." He said he had the Masters base directory and was in its base personnel office every week or so reviewing personnel lists/records so that questions like that were referred to him. When pressed again on the name Colonel Nadien, he said he "might have seen—had a vague memory of—" a colonel with a name like that.

07-26-98 The following is a summary of a joint in-person interview with Helen, Jim, and the investigators.

Jim appeared to be a recovering alcoholic and of average intelligence. During the interview he was stoic, smooth-talking, and blank-faced. Everyone present agreed he was capable of stonewalling the investigators. He remembered Helen and was cordial in his greetings. When asked about their conversation years earlier he replied, "I can't remember," allowing for the fact he actually may not remember the incident, whether by his choice or someone else's. In the sequence of the conversation, Jim then said he'd been thinking about this all week. He then followed up by the mention of his pension not stretching far enough.

On two occasions, he broke eye contact when being questioned, and at this time added short asides that only Helen would understand based on their friendship years earlier. After the interview Helen admitted Jim may have wanted to impress her in his role as a "lady's man," knowing full well her marriage was in trouble at the time. He had been a frequent house guest at Helen's and Jon's home. She felt he was fully capable of going through the interview and convincing us of whatever he wanted. In view of his years of work in dealing with people in a security capacity, we had to agree it was a possibility.

Chapter 12

The Blue Lights

Blue lights seem to have accompanied Helen throughout her life's journey. Only after repeated questioning does Helen begin to understand and reveal the significance of their visitations.

10-03-98 Regression.

Jean (J): So, what happened when you touched the blue light as a child?

Helen (H): I was told... you don't belong in the family. You don't belong where you think you do. I said, well, it doesn't matter, they take care of me. They said, but they don't love you, and I said, I know that.

10-04-98 Regression.

H: The first time I ever saw the blue light they asked if I wanted to have a baby, and I told them no, I do not want to have a baby. I'm too young. They said, we could wait. I thought that was the end of it, but it was just the beginning.

J: I want you for a moment to concentrate on your aunt who was your real mother. I want you to make contact with her eyes and I want you to ask or pull information from her concerning whether or not she had made any agreements about her life in regard to other beings, and tell me what you're aware of.

H: Yes...

J: What is it you're aware of, Helen?

H: She did make an agreement, sort of...

J: What kind of an agreement?

H: To continue on.

J: What does that mean?

H: Because her mother had made an agreement, too. She, my aunt was from that... she came out of that agreement.

J: What are you aware of?

H: She thinks she didn't have a choice. She could have, but she didn't.

J: What do you mean, she could have but she didn't?

H: She could have said no, but she was afraid. She just went on.

J: And did you come out of an agreement?

H: Yes, because I was part of her agreement, but she couldn't have any other children.

J: Are you saying, Helen, that her agreement involved you, but at no level of awareness, spiritual, physical, or mental, did you give an agreement to be involved?

H: That's what I'm saying. I guess I didn't make it clear when they asked me if I wanted to have a baby. I said I was too young. I can't have a baby. I should have said no, I do not want to have a baby, and maybe they would have understood. I didn't say it that way so, I guess I was agreeing.

J: Who was it that asked you, Helen, if you wanted to have a baby?

H: It was not something I could see, it was not a shape, not a form, it was like a presence that I could feel.

J: I want you to be there right now, feeling into that presence. I want you to see the blue light, I want you to see and feel the presence, and I want you to be aware of who it is that's speaking to you, or what it is that's speaking to you.

H: Oh, my head hurts, the light... it's... I can't see anybody, there's no shape... it's just this light.

J: Go into the light...

H: I don't feel... I don't hear anything. I just know what is coming out of it, but I don't hear it.

J: It's not necessary that you hear it, Helen. How do you know it?

H: It's put it in my mind!

J: As you're becoming aware of it, I want you to ask... what is it or who is it that's giving me this information through the light? What is the light, and who is giving me this information?

H: Um...

J: Feel yourself in its presence.

H: They want me to feel so warm and so comfortable and just accept what they say, what they want. I can't see them and they don't say who they are.

J: I want you to ask. I want you to concentrate, make contact and ask who they are... you can do that, Helen.

H: They don't want to tell me where they are, but they're not from here.

J: Do they have a name, Helen?

H: They don't tell me the name. They say I would not understand yet.

J: Did the light or the energy of these beings touch you in any way?

H: Yes. The blue light did.

J: Where did it touch you?

H: My hand.

J: And how did it feel as it touched you?

H: Kind of tingly and warm, it didn't hurt.

J: I want you to feel it now, Helen. I want you to experience the light touching your hand. You're there, re-experiencing in the moment, what happened. I want you to be aware what's happening by the touch of the light. I want you to be aware of your surroundings. I want you to tell me where you are. What do you see around you besides the light?

H: I was in that special place that I would always go to when I wanted to be alone.

J: Where was that?

H: Not very far from my house, in the woods. It had a little stream that ran through it and a lot of trees, ferns, a lot of rocks, just a little stream. My horse is there, she didn't see the light, I guess. She wasn't afraid, so I guess she didn't see it.

J: In this particular time when you were touched by the light and asked if you wanted to have a baby, how old were you?

H: I think I was eleven or twelve... eleven.

J: And how many times before had you seen the light there?

H: I don't know, maybe... five or six, maybe seven.

J: I want you to move back in time and let yourself go to the earliest memory you have of the blue light, and as you're doing that, I want you to feel yourself becoming younger... feel your body so that you can know how big you are, how old you are... tell me about that very first time.

H: I was eight. That's the first time that I saw the blue light. The other time, when they asked about the baby, I was older then.

J: What happened that very first time when you saw the light? Did it touch you then?

H: No, it didn't come too close. I could see it just a little ways away. It just kind of sat there not on the ground, but not up in the sky. It was up a little, just off the ground. It wasn't very big. I looked at it and I'm not afraid. I should be because I never saw that before.

J: Tell me when you last saw the blue light.

H: I can't remember. I don't think I saw it before. I keep seeing it....

J: What do you mean, you keep seeing it?

H: It can't be the same one. It's the same color, it looks the same and it feels the same.

J: And where are you seeing it?

H: Just before I had Carl, they said I died and they brought me back. While I was gone I saw the light and it felt the same... warm, beautiful. It wanted to pull me in, but I wouldn't go.

J: What do you mean, you died and they brought you back?

H: Pre-eclampsia, I was really, really bad and I didn't care whether I lived or died. It hurt so bad and I was so sick. I was in the hospital and they were doing all they could to keep me going, but I guess I got tired of fighting. I let go for a minute. I should have had that baby sooner, I just couldn't seem to have him. I had this problem, and finally just let go. It would have been so easy to just go, just go with the light but I wasn't ready yet.

J: Did you tell anyone that?

H: Oh, yes. I told the doctor, and he said don't talk about it, people will think you're crazy. I told my mother, she said the same thing. My husband didn't care one way or the other, but he thought I was crazy, too. Finally I didn't tell anybody because they all thought I was crazy. I was not crazy. It did happen, and that was the same light.

J: What do you think the light did at that time? Why did it come?

H: Because I needed some help.

J: And it gave you help?

H: It gave me strength to get through what I had to do. I didn't even know what that was then.

J: What is it that you know now about what that was?

H: What I'm doing now.

J: How soon after this experience was the baby born?

H: I think two or three days. I got better and they let me out of the hospital. I went home, then right back in, and that time I did have him.

J: What are you thinking about right now, Helen?

H: Thinking that this thing is so complicated.

J: I'm going to touch your knee in a moment, Helen, your left knee, and when I do, you're going to have a deeper and deeper understanding of the purpose of all of this which is happening to you. There's going to be another letting go deep within yourself... to a much greater understanding and a pulling together of all the things that have happened... there'll be no more struggling to understand... but a much deeper acceptance to just know without all of the answers, knowing they will come... and allowing yourself at a very, very deep level to tune into the original plan... and to the originator of that plan... to begin to identify with the plan... in a way that doesn't keep you separate from it... and every time or any time I touch your knee in this way, you'll go to a deeper, deeper level... of letting go into... that acceptance and that knowing... the blue light has been with you throughout your lifetime and continues to be with you... learn to speak to it and receive from it. When was the last time you saw the blue light?

H: Last spring. (Jan. 10, 1998)

J: And where were you?

H: In my home.

J: And what were you doing?

H: I had just gone to bed, turned out the lights, and I could see a blue light reflected in the bedroom window. It should not have been there. I looked outside and of course, there was nothing there. So that meant it was in the house, it was in the hallway that goes from the bedroom to the living room. I could see from the bed, I could see the reflection in the window, but I could also see a faint, shimmering light in the hallway. I got up and I grabbed my big flashlight for protection, not for light. And I walked down the hallway with my flashlight in my hand and as soon as I stepped into the hallway, it was there, about three feet away. It just kept shimmering and changing shape. I forgot about protecting myself with the flashlight and I just stood there and looked at it. It kept changing shape, folding in on itself, and it got smaller and smaller. It went away, just disappeared in front of my eyes. But after it went, I could see like little sparkly light particles in the air. Then those went out like little lights, too.

J: And how were you feeling after your visit with the blue light?

H: Really good, and not afraid. I felt really stupid with the flashlight but I just turned around and walked back into the bedroom, got into bed, and went to sleep. I don't know why I accepted that.

J: Hadn't you been accepting it all your life?

H: Yes, I had so I guess it was no different. It had a little different shape, but the light, the warmth, the color was the same.

J: What was different about the shape?

H: Before it's always been quite round, like a ball... it had depth to it, but this was kind of... well, it didn't have a shape. It had depth to it, but it was kind of amorphous, is what they call it. It kept moving around, it would be high on one side and then that would go down. Then it would be low, and be high on the other side. Not alive, but more movement than the other ones.

J: Had anything happened, Helen, that day that was different, or anything happened after you saw the light that was different?

H: I don't think so. Well, maybe, it was before I came here to see you. We'd been talking about this, Jean and I were talking, not that day but near that time... and I was concerned.

J: What were you concerned about, Helen?

H: Well, how the sessions would go, how you would feel about me. How I would feel about you. I think it was that time when the light showed up.

J: Does the light often show up when you need help or reassurance? Is that a time it shows up?

H: Well, sometimes. If that's its purpose I need it. I need it a lot more often. Maybe it's just big things... when it comes.

J: So seeing the blue light is comforting.

H: Right.

07-16-99 Regression. Blue lights at age 13.

J: Tell me what it looks like.

H: It just shimmers, it's a beautiful blue, like the sky.

J: How big is it?

H: Not very big, it changes, it moves around, it's sort of round but kind of moves in and out.

J: What do you mean, in and out?

H: It goes like in on itself and then back out. It's kind of wavy-looking, like it's alive. Not like breathing in and out, it just changes its shape so it's not quite round all the time. What's so unusual is that it shimmers, it's such a beautiful shade of blue. Even though it shimmers, it doesn't hurt your eyes. It's just soft. And it feels warm.

J: What do you mean, it feels warm?

H: It feels warm like when you get in a warm tub.

J: So the area around where the light is feels warm?

H: Yes, and how can that be? It's in the woods and even though there's sunlight, sun and shade, it's not that kind of warm. It's not warm from the sun, I don't know how to describe it. It's just a warm, comforting feeling.

After Helen touches the blue light.

J: Then just let yourself feel those tingles and that warmth. Be totally involved in the experience, touching the blue light, feeling the tingles, the wonderful feeling of it, and let yourself move very slowly into the next moment and tell me what happens.

H: I took my finger away. That was when they asked me again did I want to have a baby. And I said no, I still don't want to have a baby. I have to go to school. I thought that was a good excuse and I guess they thought so, too. They said well, that's all right. We can wait. I was younger, maybe ten. I should have been thinking... the whole thing was ridiculous. A blue light asking me did I want to have a baby... but I didn't think so then, except that I didn't want to do that.

J: So was it the first time that you saw the blue light and that you were asked if you wanted to have a baby that you touched the blue light, or was it the second time?

H: It was the second time. I guess I was braver then. I still had the feeling I shouldn't have touched it. But I couldn't seem to stop. I don't really know why it all happened.

J: Just let yourself go into the touch again, Helen, and let your-self know what happened. Let yourself move very slowly through the experience, remembering what happened.

H: That was the time when they said that I would sooner or later, I would have one... and when I did... it would look like me but it would be like them.

J: Who is them, Helen?

H: I didn't see anybody, it wasn't voices, and it wasn't eyes. It was like the thought was in my head. I wasn't saying anything, either. That's when I learned to do it with thoughts, the first time with the blue light. I learned to communicate with my thoughts.

J: And did you have ongoing communication of that kind after that as you grew up?

H: With the blue light?

J: Either with the blue light or without.

H: I didn't do it for a while, but I could do it with Marisa.

J: Tell me about that.

H: When she grew up, we could just do it back and forth over the distance. Didn't even need a telephone. We did talk on the telephone but usually it was to confirm something we'd already talked about with the thoughts.

J: Was she also aware of that?

H: Oh, yes. I'm not sure if she could do that with anyone else, we never talked about that.

J: Was there anyone besides Marisa that you could communicate that way with?

H: I can do it with the boys sometimes, my boys.

07-18-99 Regression.

J: And when you look at when the light comes, does something different usually follow what happens? Anything significant happen after you've seen the blue light?

H: Yes, always. But it does not always have to do with the project, like the time I saw it before I met you. You're involved in the project now, not that project, you're involved in my project.

J: Which is also part of....

H: It's also part of the other... so it was like a sign not to be afraid or apprehensive.

J: So besides being significant to letting you know about the project, is the blue light also a source of comfort and trust with you?

H: Oh, yes… always.

J: So it's a gift that lets you know you're guided and well helped. Helen, I want you to reach out and touch the blue light. Let it be there. Reach out and touch it because I'm going to ask you to go back in time, not forward, but back in time. So let yourself reach out now and touch the blue light, and let me know when you're touching it.

H: Hm….

J: Good. And let yourself just become one with the blue light. Feel your entire body enveloped in it. Feel the wonderful sense of well-being, wonderful healing that takes place in every cell of your body, your mind, and your spirit. And now, Helen, I want you to be fully engaged in the choice, fully aware of what's happening and tell me… what it is that you're doing and feeling….

H: I'm in the light, it's all around, it's in front…. It's all around me, but I have my own separate light. I'm… I'm aware that… I have an opportunity….

J: What is that opportunity?

H: It will be a difficult one. I can be part of awareness. I'm not sure what that means.

J: Just let yourself go to that place inside that you do know what that means, Helen. Deeper and deeper, back to the very source of being that you've carried with you from the beginning, from the very first, and let yourself know fully… what that awareness is and what your opportunity is to be a part of it.

H: They say I could be an educator, and I don't know what that means. And I'm not a teacher. I thought that's what an educator was. I'm not pressured....

J: Go to your own place of commitment and awareness, Helen. What is it that you choose to do?

H: I choose to be an educator. I do it in a way that is different.

J: What is that way, Helen?

H: I choose to be part of this project.

J: For what reason do you choose to be part of this project, Helen?

H: Because... people need to know.

J: What it is they need to know?

H: That this is not the only civilization or universe. That there are other ways to do things, to be....

J: And Helen, what it is you're being given to help you to carry through this commitment you've made?

H: Strength, I'm given the strength. I understand that it's really difficult sometimes to make some hard choices, but I have the strength to do it now... with the light now.

J: Helen, when were you first given the blue light?

H: The first time I really remember is at nine or ten years old. I remember before... when I made the commitment. When I was older, nine or ten, I didn't make the commitment. It was already done.

J: What does that mean, Helen?

H: That I made it before I was born, well, it had to be me, nobody else could make it for me.

J: I want you to ask the blue light, Helen, just ask it when it first came into your being-ness, no matter when it was.

H: It was when they took the egg from my real mother... and did something... it hurt me... they did something with me. Then I'm inside of the person I thought was my mother. It didn't hurt very long because the light was there... but the light came from my... oh... I'm so mixed up....

J: Just be with the light and it will let you know. Just become one with the light.

H: It was with my aunt, my real mother. I think somehow the light... the light stayed with me... when I went into the... they're carrying me, but now I don't remember the light until I was older... maybe I didn't need it... until then.

J: Just be with the light now. Be at inception with the light... feel the light and see the light... the way in which an embryo can see the light. Let all thoughts of why or understanding fall away. Let yourself be in the experience of knowing the light. Let all doubt and concern fall away....Helen, I want you to go back into the experience of the blue light, enveloped in the light. I want you to feel the peace and contentment... I want you to be aware of the deep satisfaction and gratitude for the work that you've done, for the bravery and the courage, for the willingness to follow through on your commitment and the willingness to bring this investigation to this place. Just let that deep appreciation and awareness of how much good work you've done fill every cell in your body, and be aware that from this moment on you are still very, very open and appreciative of any new information that will come in. There's no need to push or be afraid, or to try to analyze or figure out why this is happening, because you know why it's happening. You know that you're part of something more and you'll be given that information, that you've asked each individual person in the project to come forward with more material when it's available. You've restated your commitment to witness what you have experienced and to bring that forward as a teaching. Be aware of the fullness of your love and of your courage... and bring that same love and courage to yourself and to the healing that's taking place, and be aware that all of the work that you've done is in the process of integration, and the deep, deep healing is continuing and will continue on all levels of your being... with every breath that you take, you breathe in... love, courage, and deep appreciation for all that you've done and all that you will do. Envelop yourself in that love. Let every breath you take continue the life force within you, continue the healing process, and renew your spirit... connect you with all there is... and keep you safe... and at your own speed, taking all of the time that you need, gently begin to bring yourself back, back from all of the places that you've been today... all of the feelings and physical experiences, knowing that you are healed and healing, that you are held and safe, and that you'll bring it all back with you... So make your way back into this room... It's Sunday morning, July 19, 1999.... Feeling wonderful, healed, full of love... feeling the life force in every cell of your body... feeling the strength and the energy coming back into every cell, every bone, and every fiber of your being. And not until you're completely ready do you need to open your eyes. Welcome.

Chapter 13

Men In Black

Numerous accounts concerning interaction with extraterrestrials include mention of the famous Men in Black. In the *Reader's Digest* book, *UFO:The Continuing Enigma*, Men in Black are described on page 118 as, "men dressed in conservative dark suits, often with white shirts, black ties, and dark hats, call at the witness' home. They look like FBI agents from a Hollywood B-movie... claiming to be from some obscure-sounding government department. They usually travel in threes, frequently the third man stays in the car, while the other two conduct the interview. The cars the MIB drive are odd, too. In the classic encounter they arrive in a brand-new car, although the model in question may have been out of production for twenty years or more. They are always prestige models. The license plates, when checked out, are unissued numbers."

10-26-97 Interview with Helen about her encounter with the Men in Black.

"Their car was shiny, extremely shiny and black, and long, with long sloping fenders, and big lights. It was really a striking looking automobile. Four-door. And it had brass or gold handles on the doors. I guess it wasn't gold, it was probably brass.

"They came in threes, and I did see those men face to face. I came up the stairs to the apartment one day as they were coming down, I stood way over to the right-hand side of the stairs and they rushed down, almost knocked me over, very rude, very threatening looking.

"They were probably about 5'8" to 5'10" in height, all of them, a little variation to the height. Real stocky-built, not fat but very muscular looking. And they were wearing black suits and black hats. Their clothes didn't seem to fit right. They didn't look comfortable in their clothes. The fedora kind of hats they wore didn't look like they belonged in that time frame at all. I just sensed that they were some dangerous people.

"They had small, dark eyes, and their complexions were kind of pasty and whitish. They looked like they didn't get out in the sun enough, and had fat faces for the rest of their size. Nothing seemed to match, the clothes, the body, the face, and the aura they gave off... nothing seemed to go together."

Interview with Marisa's husband concerning the Men in Black.

"The strange gal, Raechel, and these two strange men, Marisa said she never saw it, but they came in and there was some ruckus going on... hollering and noise. She kind of got scared.

"When Marisa started really pushing for her to get out of there was when the guys in black, she described them, came up and started... she heard a bunch of noise and everything in the bedroom and then I guess basically they just pushed their way... came right in and pushed their way into there, and there was some hollering and screaming going on...

"There was something weird about the license plate, she was looking at it. She said something about it being a sedan with some weird license plates, they weren't license plates from California."

**04-20-98 Excerpt from a letter written by a former
roommate of Marisa's.**

"I do remember her saying something about odd visitors at
the apartment. Odd in that the people who came to see Raechel
were not other students like whom Marisa and I had friendships
with."

10-03-98 Regression.

J: The only time you saw those men was on the stairway?

H: It's the only time I saw the three of them, but I saw the one
head-on. Then through the windows I saw the one, just a
profile.

J: Was there anything different or unusual about the profile?

H: I thought he looked like George Raft. He had that gangster
look, Mafia hit-man look.

J: Did you ever have reason to be afraid of them?

H: Not really, they didn't threaten me. I thought that they would
push me backwards down the stairs if I didn't get out of their
way. They were coming down, two abreast and one behind,
and the stairs were not that wide. They were not giving me
any room. They looked quite intimidating. I just felt that I
would be hurt physically if I didn't move.

J: When you continued up the stairs to the apartment, who was
there then?

H: The girls.

J: Both of the girls were there?

H: Um-hm.

J: Did they mention the men having been there?

H: Marisa mentioned it, I guess you must have run into
Raechel's visitors. I said yes, but I got out of their way before
I got hurt. I had to leave within five or ten minutes at the
most. So we didn't talk about the men.

Chapter 14

Projects and Agencies

During our conversations, Helen mentioned many different "secret government projects" by name. The possible existence of some of these projects, such as MAJI, MJ-12, and MAJIC, has been controversial for many years. Some of the other projects mentioned were more obscure, but reference to most of them was found. Again, the existence of these projects has never been resolutely proven, but their speculated purposes seem relevant to Helen's explanations. These projects are presented below without any guarantees as to their veracity.

Project POUNCE-the project formed to recover all downed/crashed craft and aliens.

Project LUNA-a mining operation and alien base on the far side of the Moon.

MAJI-is the Majority Agency for Joint Intelligence. All information, disinformation, and intelligence is gathered and evaluated by this agency, and it operates in conjunction with the CIA, NSA, and the Defense Intelligence Agency. MAJI is responsible to MJ-12.

MJ-12-(standing for "Majestic Twelve") mystery was sparked off with the 1987 publication of an alleged briefing document from ex-U.S. President Truman to president-elect Eisenhower in November 1953. The document dealt with government knowledge about UFOs, aliens, and above-Top Secret projects.

MAJIC-a security classification and clearance of all alien-connected material, projects, and information. MAJIC mean MAJI controlled.

Project PLATO-the project responsible for diplomatic relations with the aliens. This project secured a formal treaty (illegal under the Constitution) with the aliens. The terms were that the aliens would give us technology. In return we agreed to keep their presence on earth a secret, not to interfere in any way with their actions, and to allow them to abduct humans and animals. The aliens agreed to furnish MJ-12 with a list of abductees on a periodic basis.

Project AQUARIUS- a project which compiled the history of alien presence and their interaction with Homo sapiens upon this planet for the last 25,000 years.

Project GABRIEL-no reference was found to this project.

Project EXCALIBUR-is a weapon to destroy the alien underground bases. It is a missile capable of penetrating 1,000 meters of tufa/hard packed soil such as that found in New Mexico with no operational damage. The device can carry a one megaton nuclear warhead.

Project GARNET- the project responsible for control of all information and documents regarding this subject and accountability of the information and documents.

National Reconnaissance Organization- The NRO designs, builds, and operates the nation's reconnaissance satellites. NRO products, provided to customers like the Central Intelligence Agency (CIA) and the Department of Defense (DoD), can warn of potential trouble spots around the world, help plan military operations, and monitor the environment.

Delta- is the designation for the specific arm of the NRO which is specifically trained and tasked with the security of these projects.

Area 51-Dreamland- is located at a corner of the Nevada Test Site, where highly classified national defense projects have been conducted for over four decades. Russian satellites have taken aerial photographs of this facility and sold them to the American public.

"Crawford" AFB- located in Lincoln, Nebraska, home of the Strategic Air Command (SAC), and the 20th Intelligence Squadron. This squadron is a subordinate organization of the National Air Intelligence Center (NAIC).

"Masters" AFB- a decommissioned Air Force base located near Sacramento, California. This base once housed a unit from SAC.

The acronym ATIC that Helen jotted down on a note, with the words Aerospace Technical Information Center written after, presented a challenge we couldn't solve. In the Acronyms, Initialisms, and Abbreviations Dictionary 1994, p. 332, ATIC has a similar sounding name, Aerospace Technical Intelligence Center. The Aerospace Technical Information Center (ATIC) is believed to be the original name of the Air Force Technical Intelligence Center (ATIC).

In response to a FOIA request, the Department of the Air Force replied in a letter dated 09-12-96, "From June 1947 through Dec. 1969 the Air Force was primarily responsible for investigating the UFO phenomena. That investigation was conducted by the Air Technical Intelligence Center (ATIC) at Wright-Patterson AFB, Ohio. That organization is currently known as the National Air Intelligence Center (NAIC)."

A thin, tenuous, and at times speculative thread seems to be connecting these projects, agencies, and places. It is wise to remember that for its size and weight, the thread of a spider's web is considered the strongest thread known to mankind.

Chapter 15

Symbols

The triangular insignia with three horizontal lines found on the food containers, water jugs, and license plates was a tangible logo that needed further examination. Searching sixteen source books on symbols ranging from symbol dictionaries, hieroglyphs, astrology, mysticism, mythology, and Chinese symbolism, a researcher found nothing definitive. A book on California license plates yielded nothing. An Internet search of the site www.symbols.com gave some hope, but not an exact match. Contacting the webmaster at this site with a query, Carl Liungman, the author of *The Dictionary of Symbols*, answered and gave some advice on how to proceed: "My tip is that you study the triangle and ideograms with lines at their bases and see which clues that may give you."

The related symbols and ideograms were found on this site, and combined to form the logo Helen drew. The resultant meaning of this combination was somewhat revealing.

A triangle can symbolize power, danger, God, the Holy Trinity, and fire. Symbols can have opposite meanings, in this case safety and success.

A triangle with one line is the most common sign for the element of air.

A triangle with two lines is the alchemists' sign for mixture.

The ideogram △ signifies similarity in one dimension. But ≙ means identity, a similarity so strong that there is no real difference.

It is quite logical that ≙ has been used in meteorology to indicate mist, i.e., an atmospheric condition where everything is identical.

The combination of these signs yields a symbol that could have the meaning signifying an organization filled with danger, and having godlike powers with those belonging identifying so strongly there is no difference.

Could the symbol seen on Raechel's food and drink containers, and on the license plates, symbolize this meaning? Could this be the purpose of the Humanization Project? Undertaking a project dealing with the genetic manipulation of the human race might be considered as assuming godlike powers. Their ultimate goal appears to be the mixing of two races creating a new race that is identical, no visible differences. The opposite sign holds true also, and could symbolize "safety" for the alien race, "success" for the project.

Chapter 16

Marisa

Marisa never lost sight of her goal to become a rehab counselor. She could have used her blindness as an excuse to give up; instead she turned it into an asset, using it as a way to reach and help others.

Marisa struggled through junior college and Golden State University. Never complaining about the inordinate amount of time necessary to do her homework, she just kept on until she was finished. With little time left for recreation she never complained about a thing.

Her acceptance of others no matter what they looked like or what they had done was illustrated time and again. From the time she saw and befriended the 'rat' baby as a young girl, she always stood up for the underdog, the underprivileged, and the lonely. She agonized over her increasing psychic abilities, and not being able to help the people she saw in trouble.

A peacemaker, she was constantly intervening in arguments and disputes between her brothers and friends. Usually she was successful in helping participants see all sides of the issue and reach a peaceful settlement. She had real compassion for the lonely. As an adult she opened her home to those away from home, with no place to go, or who would otherwise have been alone during the holidays and prepared gourmet meals for them.

The one item she kept her entire life was the picture of Jesus, given to her by her baby-sitter. The picture came to symbolize her "Bridge Over Troubled Waters," sustaining her during hard times. It was probably the one possession she treasured above anything else she ever owned.

Marisa fell in love, married, and had a child. Nothing could stop her from living the American dream. She had a goal, she was determined nothing could stop her, nothing did stop her.

Marisa's reaction to Raechel and the strange men dressed in black who visited the apartment is still remembered by her friends.

Marisa's husband.

"Marisa called Raechel strange and having problems with some of her strange friends. Marisa was frightened by at least one incident and wanted Raechel out of the apartment."

Marisa's friend and former roommate.

"I talked to Marisa about Raechel within the first month after she had departed. We had a little 'girl talk,' just the two of us, and I remember sitting on the steps outside the apartment, and being nervous and giggling about this strange experience. We were somewhat frightened, but treated it as just weird."

01-09-98 Interview with Marisa's brother Carl.

Jean (J): Did Marisa regain some of her sight?

Carl (C): She got it all back. She had a hemorrhage at the back of her eyes, and she was blind then, but before she died she could see.

J: Do you have any sense of when her sight started to come back relative to this period we're talking about, early 1972?

C: I have to say it got better right after that. I never thought about it. I was in the service and she was blind and the next thing I knew, she was seeing again.

J: And....all of a sudden she wasn't totally blind?

C: I never thought of it that way. It just got better like that, didn't it?

J: Of Marisa just before her death.

C: She was having the time of her life, she was happy, so happy, and so was he (her husband). It was just like a dream, then somebody just came along and stepped on it.

12-10-98 Synopsis of a telephone interview with an old boyfriend of Marisa's.

He had nothing but the highest praise for the work that Marisa accomplished in helping disadvantaged persons. "Marisa made a great difference in people's lives, and was an outgoing, helpful, caring person."

12-15-98 Second telephone interview with Marisa's old boyfriend.

"There was an awful lot that she could do and did do. I always remember Marisa being very realistic. The one thing that always kind of amazed me about her was that she was very accepting of what had happened. She didn't let it deter her or slow her down. She still had ambitions, goals, she wanted to achieve things and be somebody. She didn't let the visual impairment get in her way. I think she led a very full and active life at the time I knew her.

05/25/98 Interview with Marisa's husband.

"I went back to work and she started going to Golden State University for her Master's. She got everything done except for the project, which I still have all her research for."

He speaks of Marisa's psychic abilities.

"She could remember her dreams and a lot of times she would wake up and be scared. She'd start telling me about these dreams she was having, it was like she'd see things that had happened. She was there, but she couldn't do anything. She described it one time, "I saw this wreck and I was there, but I couldn't do anything about it. There was a man, and a woman, and a child in the car but I couldn't do anything." Then we get the paper and we start reading about it, the whole thing, a clipping of an accident where a man, a woman, and a child go off the road and somebody's killed. We started reading a little bit on leaving the body and stuff like that. I told her that it's possible for her to travel and that maybe she is leaving her body.

"She felt comfortable but sometimes uncomfortable because she couldn't do anything about it. She was an observer, watching what was going on, but couldn't do anything about it. The one thing we always agreed upon was if she had a bad feeling about something, we'd stop and wouldn't do it.

"If her intuition was, this doesn't feel right--okay, we're not going to do it. I felt comfortable with that. No matter what, if you say no, if your intuition tells you we're not going to do it, then we don't do it. There was an incident, we were driving back and she said, no, don't go that way...go this other way, and we did... and the next day we would read that there was an accident about that time where some people had gotten killed.

She felt frustration. I wish I could do something, sometimes she would cry because, "I couldn't do anything...I could only see them...I tried to...."

Foreseeing the unthinkable.

"There was a recurring dream that she started having, it seemed like for the last year. Then she started saying she wasn't going to be around next year. It wasn't direct enough for me. I said, 'oh, honey, you're going to still be around'. She said, no, I don't think so, and that's when we started discussing deaths and what are you supposed to do, and what I am going to do.

"We had bought a house, and were living in it. She was in her position as a teacher and we were remodeling the house. I was working on the house and she was helping with the work. Then she started dreaming more, and one recurring dream she had was waking up and telling me she was in the water and everybody was sinking, but a hand reached down to her and picked her up. And she took off walking across the water and she said... 'maybe it was Jesus, I don't know...., but a hand came down through the water and picked me up and I was able to walk across the water....' So on her gravestone it says, 'Friend, wife, mother—she could walk on water'."

Marisa's death on December 7, 1990.

"We were at my Christmas party at work, and we were sitting down with a friend. We were discussing death and my thing was that when I go, I'd like to walk out...I think the Eskimos have it right. You go out on an iceberg and let it float away and that'll be the end. We carried on this conversation because the couple that we were with, she was Native American Indian. We discussed this for a while, and then sat down and ate dinner. After dinner we were up dancing and she says, I feel kind of dizzy. I need some fresh air. So we walked out. She just kind of collapsed right there in front of me. I thought maybe she's having a reaction, I need some sugar...

"I figured the first thing I'm going to do is give her sugar and orange juice. I hollered, somebody get some help... somebody get me...and does she have a medical condition? I says, yes, she's a diabetic, get me some orange juice and sugar or sugar and water, something... and...basically I tried to give her some sugar and water and her teeth just collapsed on the glass and it just...broke it...in pieces...

"I was just trying to pour it into her throat a little bit to try to give her some sugar water. They tell me this was probably when she gulped back and everything filled into her lungs. What happened was that her lungs filled up. The way the doctor described it was heart arrhythmia and you gulp and everything goes into your lungs and fills the lungs up. There was no indication... I just feel faint. I didn't wait for the ambulance, I had a friend drive me. I tried to...I gave her mouth-to-mouth all the way to the hospital, and they told me that they took her and said they couldn't resuscitate her...that her lungs had filled up too much."

On the morning of her funeral, Marisa's students awakened with renewed knowledge, courage, and determination in their hearts. They had decided to show her their acceptance of the gift of freedom she had given them. They were no longer prisoners in their homes, always dependent on someone else. By refusing to yield to the limitations imposed by her blindness, she had inspired hope and given help to all of them. Saddened by her untimely death, her words echoed loudly in their minds, "Never give up, you can do it, set your goals high. Blindness is no more of a handicap than any sighted person saying 'I can't.' If you believe in yourself, you can accomplish anything."

She had given them the knowledge of how to get around town on the bus, how to interact with others, both blind and sighted. She had given them the courage to try and the determination to succeed. Filing into the funeral home as a group after arriving individually by bus, they knew it was what she would have wanted. It would make her happy.

05-25-98 Marisa's husband.

Have you had any sense of communication from Marisa since her death?

"Yes, I think so after her death. I don't know if it's communication or not, but sitting in the house up in Sandy Heights, it was like I said to her, I said to my son, I says, well...you know your mom's somewhere else now. I'm not religious, but I said she's somewhere else. I think she's still around. We were lying there together and I said well, honey, if you've got any kind of pull up there, why don't you let it start snowing...and it started snowing.

"The whole area got snowed on. I wasn't paying any attention to the weather and it started snowing and snowing and snowing. Finally I said, honey, if you've got any kind of pull up there, would you tell them to please stop."

Marisa's husband told those assembled at her funeral, "Not only was she a great teacher, but a wonderful wife, mother, and friend. I miss you, Marisa, we all miss you. I will always love you." With these words of goodbye, he walked over to the coffin and kissing his wife one last time, reached inside his suit coat and pulled out Marisa's favorite possession. Placing the faded, worn print of Jesus gently in her hands, he carefully closed the coffin lid.

"You know, she was a great lady...and she'll always be a great lady...."

Chapter 17

Contact With Marisa, Raechel And The Colonel

Contacting Marisa, Raechel, and the Colonel directly through hypnosis was discussed. It was decided that there would be nothing to lose, and possibly some interesting new ideas or leads to be learned. Trying to establish contact psychically sounded a bit extreme. However, June, with Helen's permission, agreed to see if she could elicit more information.

None of the three we attempted to contact, Marisa, Raechel, or the Colonel, would speak through Helen's voice. They did agree to communicate through ideomotor responses utilizing the movement of Helen's fingers. Frustratingly, this limited the questions to yes, no, and I don't know. The resulting sessions were long, and are summarized in the following pages.

Marisa.

Marisa has been trying to contact her mother through the various unusual incidents that have been happening to Helen.

Marisa confirmed the information that she was a hybrid, and knew this fact as a small child. She did not realize Raechel was a hybrid at first, but within a short time realized they were connected genetically.

She is still in contact with Raechel, who died shortly after leaving college, but not from natural causes. She was murdered by members of the military or government. The colonel, who is still alive, was aware this was going to happen and agreed it needed to be done. He did not participate in the immediate actions resulting in Raechel's death.

Marisa indicated she could communicate through her eyes. The unusual birds visiting Helen are trying to communicate with her through their eyes. She said that Helen has more information in her subconscious mind, but is not yet able to remember it.

Marisa assured us she had died of natural causes.

She indicated she has been warned not to give any further information about the colonel. She believes that she and others, including Helen, would be in danger if she reveals this information. Marisa will contact her mother when she feels it would be safe to tell more about the colonel. She wanted us to continue to investigate the case and feels the results of our investigation will be of positive use to the world.

Marisa indicates she has more information on the Humanization Project, but isn't able to tell us at this time.

Raechel.

Raechel confirmed that she had been taken from Helen's body and nurtured as an embryo in the large tanks. The colonel was her father, but he did not realize it at first. He decided to take care of her because she communicated this fact to him through her eyes. He conveyed much of the information about the base to Helen through his eyes.

Raechel said the colonel is still alive; that he was connected with, but not responsible for, her death. She had been killed about two years after leaving the apartment, because she was considered a threat to the project.

Raechel confirms she has been trying to communicate with Helen through the eagles. When Helen had refused to take care of the babies in the canisters, she had been given the job of making public the information on the project. The colonel is still involved in the project, which is still going on in the underground facility. At this time it is not safe for Helen to learn more.

Other members of Helen's family are involved in the project. The date Raechel had with Carl did not involve any sexual contact. Carl's inability to remember most of the date is because he was taken someplace or given information that made it important for him to forget the evening.

Raechel was created as a hybrid on Earth, and incubated on a spaceship. The ship left Earth and then came back when she met the colonel. Helen and the Colonel are fully human.

We explored the circumstances of Raechel's death through a regression with Helen.

07-17-99 Regression. During a regression it is learned that Raechel is no longer alive. That she died in a supposed accident.

J: What to you mean, supposed to be an accident?

H: She fell someplace... down a flight of stairs. She didn't fall, she was pushed. She didn't die right away but she was dead when they found her, when other people found her.

J: And why was she killed?

H: I'm not given that information...except she felt too much.

J: She felt too much? What do you mean?

H: She felt too much caring for me and for Marisa. She was only allowed to go so far. She went beyond the point. It wasn't time yet for that to happen.

J: What were they afraid would happen, because she felt too much?

H: They don't tell me that.

The Colonel.

The colonel does not want his true name to be known at this time. He feels it would be a danger for Helen to have this information. He is still monitoring Helen through other members of the project. He is aware of Raechel's and Marisa's contact with Helen, and is still in contact with Raechel. Although he is no longer working directly with the military, the project is still going on.

He had been taught to communicate through his eyes by the military, which in turn had been taught by the hybrids, and the ETs. People are still being taught this skill today.

The colonel no longer believes the project is for the good of mankind, but is in fact a danger. He feels if the information is made public, something could be done to halt the project. He indicated the hybrid project is being used in a way that is taking power away from mankind. Others in the military who are against this project are beginning to speak out. He does not feel the agreement between the aliens and the government is being honored, and that neither side is honoring the agreement.

He said more information would come forth after the book was written.

Nothing concrete was learned through these sessions that could be researched further. Contact with these individuals or spirits was interesting, but there was no way to verify that contact was actually made. It is included here as wait-and-see information.

Chapter 18

Currently Occurring Paranormal Events

Other than taking Raechel out on a date, Carl knows nothing of the story of Raechel and Marisa. He had recently moved to the area and was living with his mom until he found an apartment when some strange incidences occurred.

Helen continues to have experiences with the eagles which have appeared at odd times, exhibiting behaviors not indigenous to raptors. Once she saw two eagles hovering over her home as she came back from downtown. Another time two eagles kept abreast of her car for more than 100 miles as she drove through a particularly upsetting part of a journey. Eagles don't hover, and they certainly couldn't keep up with a car speeding down the highway. These events qualified as unusual, so Helen was asked whether she had ever had any other unusual experiences that she couldn't explain.

"An amorphous, shimmering light appeared in my bedroom the night my father died in 1977. He was in New York State and I was in Montana. It woke my cat which was asleep on the bed with me and she woke me and was very frightened. About three hours later, at 6 A.M., I received a call that he had died at about the same time the light appeared."

The following is a summary of some unusual events occurring since the investigation began in 1995.

An interview with Helen concerning unusual birds.

"I have a hard time at Christmas, because of my daughter's death being so close to Christmas. I was moping around Christmas morning, trying to watch the Macy's parade and cheer myself up. I noticed the big cat was sitting on the stool over by the window and was looking up underneath the overhang of the roof. I went to see what he was staring at and saw another bird like this weird thing that was at the office window a while back. It was hanging upside down, off the overhang of the roof, and was just kind of swinging back and forth. It was looking at me, but not in a piercing sort of way, it was more like it was there to cheer me up. I laughed at that one. I remember saying to it, you look so stupid, you look so stupid, but you made me laugh. It swung and it swung, and then the phone rang and I went to answer it. The bird was gone when I went back. But I know again that I didn't imagine it because the cat called my attention to it first. It isn't that my cats are so smart or anything, but they're really perceptive of anything out of the ordinary that disrupts their schedule."

06/22/98 Photograph.

Helen called and told me about a puzzling experience that occurred that morning. I urged her to write it down in as much detail as she could remember.

"I can see no logical explanation for what happened. I was gone about an hour and a half, returning at about 10:15 A.M. The minute I came into the kitchen I knew something had happened. Then just at the entry to the hallway off the living room I saw the wooden back to the picture of Marisa and her husband placed carefully and squarely on the floor. The front of the picture (glass, photo, and small picture of my grandson in the corner) was intact on the wall. When I picked the back off the floor, I realized it had a sort of lip to hold the glass in on the bottom as well as a hook on the top to hang the whole thing with, and that what was on the wall had nothing to hold it together or hang with. When I removed the glass and picture from the wall, it all slid apart and I was unable to get it together to hang back up. One cat was securely locked out on the deck and the other two were inside and acted quite nervous and didn't want to come close to the hallway or the wall for some time. They could not have carried out something like that. Both boys were at work all day (Helen's other son lived in the same town) and I had locked the house securely before I left. Nothing else had been disturbed that I could tell. When Carl came home I told him what I'd found. He took the picture apart and tried to hang it up without the back and it was impossible to do."

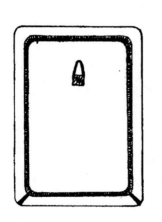 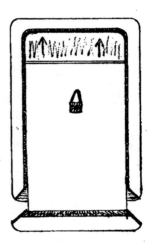

FIGURE 8. DRAWINGS OF MARISA'S PHOTO FRAME SHOWING ITS
DEISGN AND HOW IT DEFIED THE LAWS OF PHYSICS.

07-09-98.

After the photo incident whenever Helen and Carl walked into the kitchen they would look at the photo to see if anything else had happened to it. Imagine Carl's surprise when several days later the photo had started to move, once again defying the laws of gravity. During an interview with Carl, he reveals his reactions, and his attempts to explain these unusual events.

"I got accused of doing that. Mom thought I was playing a foolish trick, but I didn't. I came home and she told me that the picture, that the back of Marisa's picture was out and lying down here.

"What she did was find it lying over here on the rug and the picture was hung back up. Without the back on it. Which is pretty hard to do. I can't hardly get it on there. And then a couple of days later, the bottom of the picture was slid out, this bottom part, again... which you have to... it was slid out like that on there."

Where was it the second time you saw it?

"It was not on the floor, but the bottom of the picture was slid down. It was on the hook, and the back is on the hook. So how can it slide...the picture has to slide up... which is kind of unusual. All the other pictures were nice and straight. I checked the backs of all the pictures. I thought maybe somebody broke in and was looking for... sometimes people hide things in pictures."

Did the photos fall off the wall or anything during the big earthquake?

"No, they didn't. And that was a good earthquake."

"I had thought of poltergeist phenomenon when this happened, but nothing else was disturbed and we don't have any teenagers."

You made absolutely sure the second time when you fixed it that it was hooked on the hook?

"I most certainly did. I did it. I put it up. None of the other ones had been moved. They all had cobwebs. I'm Mr. Gotta be an Excuse for Everything... not an excuse but an answer. The top slid up. That was the bizarre part of it. I could see the hook was on the frame and the top slid up. I had to inspect everything around here to see if I could duplicate it. There has to be an answer for everything, but there isn't."

After careful examination of the photograph and frame, it was agreed that there was not a logical explanation for what happened.

Footsteps.

At 8:20 A.M., carefully locking the door behind her, Helen left to go to some garage sales. Carl was sleeping in after working late the night before. Around 8:45 A.M. as he is beginning to wake up, he hears footsteps going from the kitchen, down the hall, and to the office. He assumed it was his mom. At 9:15 A.M. the phone rings, he ignores it thinking his mom will answer it. As the phone continues to ring, Carl finally gets up to answer it. It was then he noticed the photograph of his sister had slipped up again.

C: "I thought it was mom. I thought it was her. I was sleeping in, and I thought it was grandma sneaking around the house trying to be polite like she does when I work late. She kind of tiptoes around. Then the phone rang and it rang and it rang. I jumped up and came out and answered it, and she wasn't here."

H: But I'd been gone for quite some time.

C: "I got up because she didn't answer it. I figured, well, she must be out in the garden. I answered the phone and went out and looked for her. She wasn't there. Then I looked in the garage and the car was gone. She snuck right out on me. I thought it was her, I really did. I was really surprised when I came out and nobody was here. Very surprised."

06-22-98.

In the afternoon of the day the photograph came off the wall, Helen was listening to part of an earlier regression when she experienced yet another strange event.

"Off and on during the afternoon I would catch various scents throughout the house—pipe tobacco, chocolate, allspice, and perfume like Marisa used to wear. I don't own any of Marisa's perfume. No one in the neighborhood smokes a pipe, and I hadn't been cooking. The event affected me quite deeply, more than it really should have, and I felt quite agitated, much like the reaction from the eagles and other birds. There certainly wasn't anything threatening about it, just a real attention-getter."

Caller ID.

As the result of some nuisance calls, Helen purchased a caller ID device. She hooked it up, and it worked as advertised, for about a week. Then perhaps a chance request by Carl evokes a mysterious response by the machine.

Carl (C): Well, we were discussing if it was Marisa, or somebody was causing the falling photo. I said, "Leave a message in writing." I'd like to see something in writing on the bathroom mirror, like when you take a shower and you come out and you see something on the.... The phone rang, and the caller ID printed out, not a name, but, "Saturday June 29."

Helen (H): It happened on June 29th, the date was correct, but it showed Saturday. It printed out Saturday when it was really Monday?

C: And it printed out like somebody had called you, how they print the name out, it's in that spot, which is bizarre. I asked for a sign in writing, so we waited around for Saturday to happen.

H: Nothing happened?

C: Nothing happened.

H: I checked with the local repair service and nobody seemed to know much. They think the batteries went dead, but they said they never heard of the days of the week being printed out, and suggested I call U.S. West. I called their troubleshooter, and he'd never heard of that, either. The batteries weren't dead.

11-07-97 Helen sees the insignia again.

"I had just received some meditation tapes. I was really all upset because the boys had a lot of personal problems and they'd both dumped them all on me. I was just beside myself, so I thought, well, this is a good time to put on this tape, and I'm just going to lie down and listen. I won't have to deal with the problems for a while. I was playing this tape and I guess I did go into an altered state of consciousness, which you do with some of these tapes.

"I felt really fine, but I thought I was looking through a window. The first thing I saw... it was like looking out from the dark in through a lighted window, and I saw this trilateral insignia, but instead of being with the base on the bottom it was upside down. I looked at it, and I thought this is so strange, and this is not right. Then nothing else happened that I remember except I drifted for a little bit. Then I looked through another window and I could see the face of one of these men in black. I know it's the face that I saw originally. He looked like George Raft, wasn't he kind of a mobster/gangster type?"

Eureka Entities.

During her first regression, Helen referred to some strange-looking people watching her while she is dining at a restaurant in Eureka, northern California. She remarks that other people don't seem to notice how odd-looking they appear. Exploring this occurrence a bit further enabled Helen to better recall the experience and sketch the entities.

05-01-98 Helen describes the encounter in a note.

"The two of them looked identical. I saw them on September 20, 1996, in Eureka, northern Califronia, just outside a restaurant, at approximately 6:30 P.M. The entities walked deliberately to the window at my side and stared at me for approximately thirty to forty-five seconds. Then they entered the restaurant and sat at a table about fifteen feet away. They continued to stare at me. The waitress and I were apparently the only people to see them as the other diners appeared totally unaware of their presence.

"They were about 5' 10" tall, very thin, with disproportionately long arms and legs for the rest of their bodies. They walked stiffly, mechanically, in lockstep with abnormally long strides. Dressed in matching two-piece, sky-blue jogging suits with helmets, similar to bicycle racing helmets, on top of their heads.

"Their faces were elongated, egg-shaped, with the appearance of being artificially constructed. Their faces were covered with irregular patches of skin or with scales. My first impression was that of a botched plastic surgery, however, both their faces were identical. The color of the patches or scales was light brown, in variegated shades.

"Their eyes were like upright teardrops, very dark brown with a piercing gaze. They were solid brown with no pupil, iris, or white visible. Their ears were not distinguishable under their close-fitting helmets. The side surfaces of their heads appeared flat.

"They exhibited no change in expression on their faces during the ten minutes or so that I observed them. They seemed very ill at ease inside the restaurant and they did not move in their seats once they sat down. "

Helen Tells of a Birthday Phone Call.

On my first birthday following Marisa's death, she'd been on my mind all day. I'd just gotten into bed that night when the phone rang in my office across the hall. Upon answering it I heard Marisa's distinctive voice say, "Hi, mom. I just wanted to let you know that I'm all right." Sure that someone was playing a cruel joke on me, I replied through tears, "Don't do this to me, this isn't right." As if the voice hadn't heard me, it continued, "I'm okay, mom, I just wanted you not to worry about me." Then there was a lot of hissing and crackling sounds like radio static, which gradually faded to complete silence and no dial tone. I slowly hung the phone up, picked it up again, and the normal dial tone had returned. I know that somehow Marisa had found a way to communicate with me electronically in this one-way conversation.

The Van.

On May 22, 1998, Helen and her son are having breakfast together one cloudy, rainy morning when they both get up to refill their coffee cups. Glancing out the window, they are surprised to see an official-looking van drive up and park, not in the driveway or at the curb, but on an unused strip of land adjacent to the front lawn. The van parked facing the kitchen window, and two sinister-looking men wearing sunglasses stared at the startled mother and son standing inside.

In the ten years Helen has lived at this address, only a handful of cars have parked in this spot. None have ever elicited the response this van did. In recounting the visit, both Helen and Carl have that telltale slip in logic that could indicate something more has happened than can be consciously remembered.

Helen and Carl are interviewed about the incident while it's still fresh in their minds.

06-06-98 Interview with Carl giving a description of the van and its visit.

"It was in the morning, probably 9 o'clock. My mother and I had just walked out to the kitchen and looked out the window when the van pulled up and stopped. There were two gentlemen in there.

"The men in the van looked like a couple of pilots, almost, real clean-cut, real concentrated. They just beaded in on us, just like we beaded back on them. I think they were 100%, the focus was on us in that kitchen. They had sunglasses on. I thought they had dark green uniforms on. They were both dressed the same. It wasn't like a regular military uniform... it was all over so quick.

"They had nothing in their hands at all. It was really strange because we had just walked out to the kitchen to get coffee. We just looked out the darned window and it was pulling up. They just stopped and looked straight at us.... I mean eye-to-eye contact. It was really kind of bizarre. I was going, what have I done wrong? What have you been doing wrong? It sort of looked like FBI, like an agency or something on that line. They just looked real professional, clean-cut. They kind of looked like pilots, with the glasses on, and really strange.

"They just stared at us, we stared at them, and then they backed up and turned around and took off.

"I felt pretty strange, just looking out the window and seeing a van like that pull up, and they did have their lights on. Then for them to stop and turn their heads in unison and look straight at us... looking in... made me feel pretty uncomfortable. I was trying to think, well I haven't done anything wrong, of any magnitude, and I know my mother doesn't do anything wrong.

"Their heads turned straight towards us. If they weren't staring at us, they'd be looking straight ahead instead of turning their heads to the left and looking towards us. And both their heads turned at the same time, made eye contact with sunglasses. Contact, how's that? You could feel that focus, you can feel when someone's looking at you. Just as quick as they pulled up and looked at us and we looked at them, they proceeded on their way. Not fast… just kind of moseyed on out of there. Then mom went to see if she could find them a couple of minutes later. They were no place to be found. They just looked too professional, sort of like a cross between a pilot and FBI, you know clean-cut… just real sharp… straight upright. They weren't sitting like I am….

"On the back of the van was a sign saying 'Caution. This vehicle makes frequent stops.' And the license plate started with an E, the same size as the numbers. The plate was orange, like the old Oregon license plates. The new plates aren't orange like that. It looked like an older plate on a new Dodge or a Plymouth full-size van. It didn't make sense because all new vehicles, you've got Oregon Trail, they've got three different kinds of plates, and they're not just basic orange with the black letters. Those are plates that are on older vehicles like twenty years ago… ten to fifteen years ago. The Oregon plates, you don't see them any more unless they're on an old vehicle and you buy it. Then when you re-license it, they give you the new plates.

"There were no markings at all on the van, other than the outdated license plate. It wasn't a private vehicle because I didn't see a sticker up in the right or left-hand corner for your registration.

"The plate looked like it was a state or government plate because it didn't have the little renewal stickers on it, just the E without anything in either corner.

"The color of the van was blue or silver. I've got to remember things when I see them like that or write them down. It's like when you're dreaming and you wake up and it's fresh in your memory, and five minutes later you wash your face and you want to tell somebody what you... forget it... it's gone. They were there couple of minutes at most.

"Police lights? Heavens no, there weren't any lights on that car. There was on top, but they weren't red and blue, they were all white. They went across the top of the van, on the top of the roof, about a third of the way back. They ran all the way across, and they were all clear lights."

Helen and Carl describe the visitors and the van.

Carl (C): Both the same, like the Bobbsey Twins.

Helen (H): They looked like goons, is what my impression was.

C: Like Joe Friday and his partner.

H: No, a lot worse than that, much worse. They had dark brown hair.... Nothing was quite right about it. They didn't turn the motor off. They looked in the kitchen window as if they were expecting us... which was the first time the two of us had stood in the kitchen window at the same time since I can remember. It was if they had sort of orchestrated the whole thing, and there we were and there they were, and they were just going to give us a stare-down. They just pulled in and looked directly in, they knew exactly how far to pull in so they would get that proper angle. It was as if they looked in and grabbed me, that was how I felt.

C: They looked in and they were looking for us. It was kind of powerful in a way. Just as quick as they locked on, they locked off, made like we weren't there any more, and just drove off.

H: They didn't look away at all.

C: Yeah, when they drove off, they weren't turning around or looking, or anything, like robots. We did what we came for and that's the end of that and they weren't looking at any other houses. That was the strange part, you'd think they'd come up and knock on the door, talk to somebody, or say, we're looking for so and so. There was none of that.

H: Well, those people were military of some kind or government.

C: You can't have a newer vehicle with one of the old plates like that, they're outdated, they don't use them any more. It wasn't labeled "First Presbyterian Church bus" or "Operation Head Start" or U.S. Navy, there was no labeling at all on it. They may have a "frequent stops" sign if they had a bus or something. It was just totally out of character, no insignia or a logo on the doors, nothing on it. That was the strange part, to have the one sign and the government plate.

H: And the E on the license plate seemed too big, the same size as the numbers.

C: I looked at one of the police cars and the E's a little bit shorter, down-centered, from the top and bottom. It's smaller, the E is smaller, not the same size.

H: I don't know why those men impressed me so much except I've seen that I've seen the eyes before, which doesn't make any sense as I'm saying it, but I have just the same. I've seen that same kind of face... really sharp, not thin, but just... chiseled, I guess you might say, sort of like George Raft used to be.

C: I thought the plate was a little extra long, a little oversize. I'd like to think that there was another number or two in it.

10-03-98 Helen is regressed to see if she can recall any details concerning the slip in logic she admits, but cannot explain.

June (J): How could you see his eyes when he wore sunglasses?

Helen (H): I don't know, but I could... you can't see through sunglasses... but I could see his eyes... and the glasses were
black... real dark... I don't know how I could do that.

J: I'm going to count from one to three, and on the count of
three, I want you to know if you had ever seen the men in the
van without their glasses on. One, two, three.

H: The passenger I don't think I have, but the driver... his eyes
were the same as the colonel's. They were a different color...
how... how... I don't know, sometimes they're black and
then I see the same eyes and they're a real bright shade of
blue. I don't know... one person, how can they change the
color of their eyes like that? It felt like it was the colonel
looking at me through those sunglasses.

10-04-98 Regression.

J: I want you to move in your experience to the men themselves. I want you to go to their eyes, the way in which you
know and have been able to go to their eyes through their
glasses, through the windshield, and just let yourself be looking directly into the men's eyes... and as you do that.

H: They want to pull me in, but I won't go.

J: Where is it they want to pull you?

H: I don't know, but they want to pull me in. It's like I can feel
somebody pulling on me physically. I won't go... I don't have
to because I'm not alone today.

J: Have you had to go before when you were alone?

H: With the colonel... but I don't have to go, because Carl's here
and he won't let me go. He doesn't know what's happening.... He knows something is wrong.

J: Is there any other way to go without going physically?

H: Oh, yes.

J: Tell me about that.

H: They can pull my mind right in, but this time I won't let that happen. I know what they're trying to do. I know what they're there for and I'm not going to go.

J: Have you ever gone there in your mind with any of the men from any of the vans?

H: No. I don't know what they want. I don't know what they want with me and I'm really afraid. I was not afraid of the colonel.

J: What's the difference here? Why are you afraid of these men?

H: I feel that they're very dangerous. I feel if I go with them... I won't come back.

J: Does that mean you won't come back physically? Or your mind won't come back? Or what is it that won't come back?

H: Well, they can't take me physically... but they can change my mind... to... I... I don't want to think like they do.

J: Who told you they could change your mind?

H: Nobody has told me, but I know they can. I don't know how I can know that, either.

J: Just be in that place right now where they are asking or pulling at your mind... just knowing that you can say no, but being at that place... I want you to ask them and I'm going to count from one to three, and on the count of three, I want you to ask what it is they're going to do with your mind. One, two, three.

H: They do not want me to tell what I know, and *I will tell what I know.* They can't harm me; the driver tried really, really hard and he was angry. I know he was angry because I resisted and he couldn't pull my mind in. I won't let him do that.

J: So something was different about the driver and the men in the van and the colonel.

H: Oh, yes.

J: What was that difference?

H: I don't believe the colonel meant me any harm.... I believe he... he had to do certain things. He had to... do the things he did... I think he had no choice... but he would not harm me, and I knew that. I felt that.

J: You said when he pulled you into his eyes, he gave you information.

H: Yes.

J: Did he also take information?

H: I don't think so. I don't think he did, he was not a cruel man, but the man in the van could be. He knew that he couldn't take me physically because I had someone else there. I think he just wanted... he would like me to change my mind and I will not change my mind.

07-16-99 Regression.

J: Have you ever looked into the windows of eyes similar to those that pulled in?

H: Not really... the eyes were not the same, but the colonel... he didn't really pull me into his eyes. He told me a lot of things with his eyes, but the men that came in the van, the first time... the one man... the driver was trying to pull me in.

J: And how did you stop him from pulling you in?

H: I just told him he couldn't have me. I was not going with him. That he could try as hard as he wanted, but I'm not going with him. Because if I went, I wouldn't be back.

J: How do you know that?

H: He told me that.

J: What did he say?

H: He said you've gone too far.

J: What did he mean, Helen?

H: The project. I told him I haven't gone nearly far enough. I'm going to go all the way, and I'm not going with you. This

time there's somebody else here and they saw what you're trying to do. He can't stop you, but he'll know what happened.

J: Who was that, Helen, that he saw?

H: It was my son, Carl, he was scared, really frightened... he
really didn't know what happened and I've never really told
him. I told him they were here because of what we're all doing,
I didn't go into any detail. I told him it was a courtesy call from
the government to try and make me back off. I told him I'm
not going to do it.

07-17-99 Regression.

Helen: I don't know what they were, you couldn't tell. I'm not sure
they were military, but they looked it... they were enforcers.

Was this a visit from two men lost in the neighborhood? If so,
why didn't they look at a map, or ask directions of the two inside
the house? Was it part of the so-called intimidation tactics of the
Men In Black, only this time they wore green?

Lightning.

In August 1999, Helen experienced severe difficulty in breathing. She managed to call 911 and ask for help. The paramedics came
and transported her to the hospital emergency room where the doctor examined her. He explained she'd had an arrhythmia attack,
(one of the listed causes of Marisa's death), a condition in which her
pulse rate had accelerated to a dangerous level. The condition is seri-
ous and the doctor prescribed an appropriate medication. As the
weeks went by Helen still had some pain, felt weak and listless. Late
one afternoon during a thunderstorm, Helen was in her office and
heard a loud crash at the window. The window rattled and the floor
shook. A blue streak of light went through the window and across
the room. She immediately smelled ozone and then had a tingling

feeling in her legs. She got scared, thinking this was it, she was going to die. All of a sudden a concussion wave hit her chest, quite hard, making her heart go thump. She continued to smell ozone for a few minutes, then it went away. The lingering pain in her chest disappeared and she's felt better, although not entirely well ever since.

Neither her computer nor any of the electrical equipment in the room was damaged. The home has underground wiring, with no power poles.

During her last regression, Helen and June were just starting the questions when something outside caught my eye. Out of their line of sight, a huge eagle dove down between her house and the neighbor's. Its wingspan momentarily cast a shadow filling the living room picture window, then it flew on. A few moments later one of the two plants hanging side by side next to the window began to sway. Not wanting to disturb the session in progress, I motioned to another person in the room to look. We both spent the next fifteen minutes trying to come up with a rational explanation for why one plant was swinging in a foot-wide arc, while the one next to it remained still.

Glowing.

A few days later Helen was talking to some friends in her front yard when suddenly the conversation stopped. The two women visitors were staring at Helen. One woman turned to the other and asked, "Do you see that?"

Helen, wondering what they were looking at, turned to see what was behind her. The women said, "No, no, not behind you, it's you. You're glowing."

Helen tried to convince the women that she wasn't glowing. The women were not convinced and left shortly thereafter.

Helen Tells About a Casino Episode.

Marisa and I had a tradition to go gambling on our birthdays whenever possible. On one of my birthdays a few years ago, I felt Marisa was very close and decided we should have our usual celebration at a nearby casino. The entire time I played the nickel slots I could feel her presence. A little after 11 A.M., hungry after having skipped breakfast, I was the first and only one in line for brunch. I handed a twenty to the Native American cashier and she asked if I was also paying for the young blonde lady behind me. I turned to see who was there, and seeing no one, told her, no, just for myself. The cashier's face blanched and she said, "I'm sorry, I must have made a mistake." I'm sure Marisa had been present momentarily in visible form just to reinforce what I'd known all morning—she was there for our customary birthday celebration.

Chapter 19

Epilogue

After five years of intensive investigation, visits to the college, the state library, hometowns, military bases, countless interviews, regressions, numerous book and Internet searches, all leads were exhausted. Despite eyewitness testimony attesting to the existence of Raechel and the colonel, on paper they did not exist.

In complete frustration, a private investigation company was hired. Their ad read, "No matter who you are looking for, we can help you find them. Our extensive data bank of information allows us to locate missing persons. Unlike other services that simply provide a list of names, we actually locate the person you're seeking." Better yet, they offered a "No Find-No Fee" guarantee.

A few days later, the company called saying, "We're sorry but you must have given us a wrong name, or perhaps you spelled it incorrectly."

When assured that the name was spelled correctly, they replied, "Are you sure? Either you're mistaken or it's a bogus name. We cannot find anyone with this name. Not in the entire United States."

"Well, we couldn't find anyone with that name either."

"It's not the same. You see, we have extensive databases and resources. This is what we do, we find people. Never, never in the history of our company have we come up with absolutely nothing.

With that they hung up.

We recalled the former intelligence officer telling us, "Doing extensive research and finding nothing is an answer, too. Never forget, 'no' is an answer, too."

Helen's heart arhythmia problem had worsened during the last couple of years and finally her doctor recommended surgery. She was quite worried about her upcoming operation. A few days before her surgery, she awakened to the sound of her cats frantically sneezing and the fragrance of Marisa's perfume permeating the room. Helen does not have any of this type of perfume in her home.

The morning after her operation Helen awakened early in the hospital. She was appreciative of the flower arrangements sent to her. A brightly-colored balloon floated in the window, a little weight attached to its string keeping it from drifting around the room.

No one came into the room, no fans came on, and no windows or doors opened. When she walked out of the bathroom she noticed the balloon had moved. It was at her bedside, with the weighted string wrapped completely around her bed rail.

I spent the first night home with Helen after her surgery, sleeping in the guest bedroom adjacent to the hallway. During the night I awakened to the sound of footsteps walking down the hall. I assumed if she needed help she would come in and tell me. I waited and when she didn't come in, I drifted off to sleep again. During breakfast I asked her if she had had a problem during the night. She replied that she felt wonderful and other than her cats being unusually restless, she had slept through the entire night.

The next day while working in her office she noticed her sleeping cats perk up and look towards the hall door. Turning down the tape she was listening to, she heard footsteps coming down the hall. Thinking it was Carl, she waited for him to come into the room. But Carl was at work across town. There was no one there.

Our investigation at a standstill, we decided to go with what we had, albeit a little circumstantial in parts, factual in others; but we felt we had built a compelling case for the validity of Helen's story.

Then, one day, while finishing up the investigation a letter arrived from an obscure department at the girls' college. It read: "This is official verification that Raechel Nadien was a student at our college in the spring semester. She was granted a leave of absence at that time." The year of attendance was also noted on the embossed college stationery. Tangible proof at last.

Several months later the department that sent us the note was contacted for further information. The woman who had signed the letter had been transferred. As far as the college was concerned Raechel had never attended the school.

In the early 1970s, when Marisa and Raechel were room-mates, cloning, in vitro fertilization, DNA manipulation, and gene splicing were topics of wild conjecture and science fiction. Today they are facts of life and we wrestle with the ethic and moral issues concerning these scientific breakthroughs.

Thirty years ago, secret underground military facilities were figments of overactive imaginations. Today, satellite photographs of Area 51 are sold on the Internet. The revelation and subsequent admission of the government's involvement in the Tuskegee and other clandestine experiments confirms the fact of unsolicited, unwanted and, at the time, unknown secret military intervention in the lives of humans.

Watching the space shuttle landing on a dry lakebed in Nevada or California reminds us that others could land there, too. Screen memories and hypnotic blocks are only a step beyond a Las Vegas stage show act. Drugs are routinely used by doctors to help their patients forget the trauma of their operations. Native American and other cultures have legends and folklore telling of star people. Go to the desert, away from the city lights. Watch as myriads of stars, planets, and galaxies shine in the night sky, signaling, assuring us we are not alone.

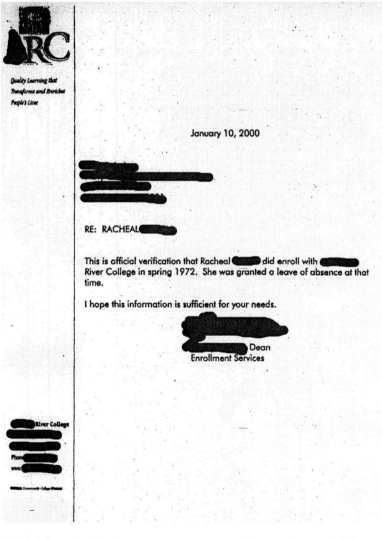

January 10, 2000

RE: RACHEAL

This is official verification that Racheal ▮▮▮ did enroll with ▮▮▮ River College in spring 1972. She was granted a leave of absence at that time.

I hope this information is sufficient for your needs.

Dean
Enrollment Services

FIGURE 9. OFFICIAL COLLEGE LETTER VERIFYING RAECHEL'S ATTENDANCE THERE.

For years rumors have hinted at government scientists working with ETs, crashed spaceships, back-engineering, human-alien hybrids, ETs eating green liquid food, and of humans having been given psychic gifts, enabling them to communicate with ETs.

When man first stepped on the moon, his ties with earthbound thinking were loosed. Gazing heavenward, the astronauts saw Earth as she assumed her place in the cosmic family. Humankind's macrocosm suddenly became a microcosm in the universe.

Eyes are said to be the windows to the soul. Raechel's eyes are not only the windows to humanity's soul, but to a universal soul.

Helen's story may be the answer to why we don't see a spaceship landing on some world leader's lawn. We have already assumed our place in the cosmos and are standing side by side looking heavenward together. Raechel is not only Marisa's sister, she is our sister, too. We are them, they are us.

Granite
Publishing
Group

To receive a free catalog that includes the *Raechel's Eyes* double-volume set as well as many other fine books, please write to...

Granite Publishing Group
P.O. Box 1429
Columbus, North Carolina 28722

to order call during business hours...
800.366.0264

or order securely on-line at our web site...
http://5thworld.com/Raechel

or email us at...
orders@5thworld.com

Thank you.